NORMISM

The Philosophy
of
Norm Macdonald

MAX WEST

NORMISM
The Philosophy of Norm Macdonald

ISBN: 9798772121191

www.logicalmeme.com

DEDICATION

To Norm, that old chunk of coal, wherever he may be.

Contents

ONE - Personal Life 1

The Secret Illness 1

The Secret Early Years 2

Quick Ascent to Stardom 5

Norm Being Norm 8

Gambling 13

TWO - Comedic Style 16

The Comedian's Comedian 16

Influences 18

The DGAF Mark Twain 21

Meta-Comedy 23

Embracing the Bomb 24

THREE - A Favorite Late Night Guest 26

Chairman of the B-O-R-E-D 27

The Moth Joke 28

Jacques De Gatineau 32

Final Letterman Appearance 33

FOUR - Philosopher-Fool 35

Anti-Intellectualism 35

Philosophy Jokes 37

Professor of Logic Joke 38

Deeply Closeted Liar's Paradox 40

What is it Like to be a Chicken? 41

Intuitionism 43

FIVE - Litterateur 47

Literary Influences 47

Meeting Bob Dylan..52

Based on a True Story 54

SIX - Politics **58**

Cultural Politics (Against Wokeness)..............................62

Against Confessional Comedy..64

Against Identity Politics 66

Jewish Jokes 68

#MeToo Controversy 72

Male Humor..74

SEVEN - Religion...**76**

EIGHT - Death..**82**

Works Cited...**90**

Preface

I saw Norm Macdonald perform stand-up at least a half dozen times over the years, far more than I've ever seen any other stand-up comedian, and any time he came through my area I made it a point to get tickets. Given his lifelong battle with cancer (aka the "battle cancer"), it now makes sense why, when I last saw him in 2018, a year in which he spent a marathon forty four weeks on the road, Macdonald ended the show by uncharacteristically telling the audience, in a most genuine and heartfelt way, how much he loved us all and how much he loved doing what he does: making us laugh.

There was an awkward moment of silence in the room after he said this. Nobody, myself included, was expecting him to say anything like this. In that brief window of time before the audience eventually began clapping, I felt an urge to respond, and came so very close to yelling "We love you, Norm!", an urge I'd never felt before in any social context, but my instilled sense of decorum prevented me from doing so. I regret that. None of us in the audience had any idea he was suffering from cancer. And yet that moment, for reasons I'll never fully understand but which I'll never forget, resonated with me profoundly and shook me to the core.

I had tickets to see him in the fall of 2021, for a show that was to take place a short time after he passed. A couple of weeks later, when I received my refund for the tickets, I shed some tears yet again over his passing and began writing this manuscript. This project began with my wanting to read everything written about Norm, to go down the YouTube "rabbit holes" that so many talk about and watch his myriad of appearances on various shows, and to understand why this man's death affected me as deeply as it has.

As part of this goal, I sought to deconstruct what made Norm 'Norm'. In the process of my research, I found sides of him I was not expecting. He was a child prodigy who carefully crafted a 'dumb guy' persona, and what was also largely hidden from public view was his Christianity, his cultural conservatism, and how well-read he was in literature, philosophy, and theology, all of which he would subtly weave into his material. In short, he was a far more intelligent man than he generally led us to believe.

A substantial portion of this book is extended quotations from Macdonald himself, touching upon subjects ranging from the nature of comedy, to culture and politics, to religion and death. Some I have transcribed from his stand-up routines and from radio and video interviews he did over the years, while others are from various print and online interviews and profiles he participated in. While I do provide interpretation and analysis throughout the book, in some places I felt it was better for me to get out of the way and let Norm do the speaking.

As it has been for countless Norm fans around the world, myself included, his death was completely unexpected and our reactions to his passing -- the depths of our grieving for a man most of us never met personally -- have been unexpected as well, moving us profoundly.

Among his fans, Norm's everyman persona engendered a sense of relatability and connection. He was more than just a comedian telling jokes, he embodied his material in such a way that the comedy and comedian were one and the same.

He will be greatly missed.

ONE

Personal Life

Norm Macdonald kept his personal life and past largely hidden from public view. Nonetheless, from various sources we can glean certain salient aspects of his life that shaped the man and his humor.

The Secret Illness

On September 14, 2021 the comedy world lost a legend: the great Norm Macdonald, who at the age of 61 died after living with leukemia for close to a decade, something he'd kept hidden from even his closest friends. "He kept it quiet because he didn't want it to affect his comedy," his brother Neil said. "He didn't want it to affect the way he was perceived … He wanted to carry on. He took great pains to conceal it from everybody but family." (CBC News, 2021). During an interview promoting his anti-confessional, semi-fictional memoir *Based on a True Story*, Macdonald expressed contempt for the narcissism of public confessionals, cryptically saying: "The brave thing to do if you have cancer is to not talk about it...is to just have it, and keep it a secret, and don't burden anyone with it. All you're doing is burdening people with those things" (Gordon, 2017). Upon his death, Macdonald's longtime producing partner and close friend Lori Jo Hoekstra observed: "He was most proud of his comedy. He never wanted the diagnosis to affect the way the audience or any of his loved ones saw him. Norm was a pure comic. He once wrote that 'a joke should catch someone by surprise, it should never pander.' He certainly never pandered" (Evans, 2021).

In an interview early in his career, Macdonald revealed (but would never discuss publicly again) that he had stomach cancer as early as 1986 and spent a year recuperating (Brownstein, 1991). From that point onward, he would deflect any indications that he was suffering from the disease. For example, the preface to a 2016 interview with Macdonald may contain an example of his deception on the matter: "Dressed in a dark-blue tracksuit and snacking on an orange and a couple apples, the 56-year-old Canadian was in an expansive mood, and a little drowsy from the antibiotics he was taking…" (Marchese, 2016).

After Macdonald's death, comedian and close friend Jeff Ross said "To think he was so sick with cancer for so long and didn't tell even his closest friends makes me so sad. (He did tell one of our close friends recently that he'd also had cancer as a kid") (Ross, 2021). One former stand-up comic who knew Macdonald back from his early stand-up days writes: "To the best of my knowledge he had [cancer] three times, but it could have been more" (O'Brien, 2021).

Macdonald's concerted effort to hide his condition from the public is, in many ways, a gauge of how much he believed in and respected the purity of comedic form.

The Secret Early Years

Born in Quebec City to parents who were both teachers, Macdonald says that as a young boy he had a "crippling shyness" which intensified upon him being identified as gifted and skipping two grades, making him both the quietest and the smallest boy in his class (Munroe, 2016).[1] In a 2011 interview, Macdonald recounts how he was largely shaken out of his extreme social anxiety when asked one day to take a blind friend of his father's shopping. The man wanted Macdonald to describe everything they encountered on the trip, everything that surrounded them, even the most banal things such as the grass  or a lamppost. The experience profoundly affected Macdonald. "Instead of always looking inward," he says, "I was looking outward" (Maron, 2011).[2]

---

[1] See also MacPherson (2012) and Grignan (1991).

[2] This interview is noteworthy for bringing to light some of Macdonald's psychological idiosyncrasies. He says that he has never learned to drive a car and that he has experiences Stendhal Syndrome (a type of panic attack that occurs after

While he deliberately projected an air of anti-intellectualism and aw-shucks simplicity in his public persona, it appears that Macdonald was much more complicated. He graduated Gloucester High School in Ottawa at age 14, and at age 16 enrolled at Carleton University in Ottawa (Grignan, 1991) where he appears to have received a degree in mathematics.[3] At one point (around the 17:00 marker) in his stand-up special *Hitler's Dog, Gossip and Trickery* (2017), after delivering a punchline involving him faux-calculating an equation, he adds as a rejoinder: "I knew that advanced math degree would come in handy one day." Of Macdonald, friend and former SNL cast member Jon Lovitz noted "He was a math genius." In the same interview, Lovitz recounts how he witnessed Macdonald being banned from a casino for card-counting.[4]

Macdonald also appears to have enrolled in Algonquin College's Broadcasting-Television program, but did not complete the course.[5]

---

being overwhelmed by what the subject perceives as great beauty). Elsewhere, he has noted his OCD behaviors, and there is of course his chronic gambling addiction.

[3] See Brownstein (1991), Gabriel (2021), and Giovannone (2021). Macdonald is listed on Carleton University's 'Famous Alumni' page (https://alumnius.net/carleton_university-838-151). One source states that Macdonald studied philosophy at Carleton University (Giovannone, 2021).

[4] *The Rich Eisen Show*, September 15, 2021, https://youtu.be/i14KjBCbSI0.

[5] https://www.thecanadianencyclopedia.ca/en/article/norm-macdonald. Macdonald's older brother, Neil, a senior correspondent for CBC News, is a graduate of the Algonquin College program.

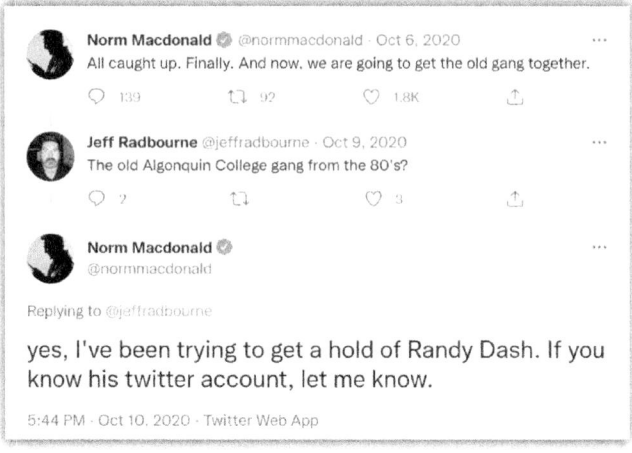

After his college experiences, he worked a series of jobs before venturing into the world of stand-up comedy. He would often claim that these were a series of manual labor jobs, occupations he greatly respected (and some might say romanticized). He says he tarred roofs and worked on an oil rig.[6] He says he once worked as a garbage collector for a couple of days (Duignan-Cabrera, 1995) and as a logging chokerman, the latter a dangerous occupation which involves wrapping a cable around a felled log which is then lifted by heavy machinery (Edgers, "Norm Macdonald Book Tour" interview, 2016).[7] In *Based on a True Story*, he highlights what might be called the silver-lining of such manual labor: one doesn't have to think too hard; the body is on automatic pilot but the mind is never inactive:

> I specialized in unskilled labor, and I was good at it. Skilled labor appealed to a different sort. It was for the thinking men. Men who liked to use their heads as much as their bodies. I didn't like to use my head, but I loved unskilled, manual

---

[6] *The Sarah & Vinnie Show*, Interview with Norm Macdonald, September 23, 2008, https://www.youtube.com/watch?v=zSQj2HIpA7Y&t=1265s.

[7] These claims may be true, but he also once revealed he worked at an insurance company (Matthews, 2016). He also reportedly crewed a ship in the Caribbean and sold magic mushrooms on Vancouver Island (Giovannone, 2021). Given his intelligence and aptitude for math, it's likely he worked more white collar jobs than blue collar jobs.

labor. That kind of work let my mind alone, let it be free. If my job was to shovel and shovel until eight hours had passed, then my body worked on its own. It had no use for my mind. So my mind would take off to a world of imagination. And that's where stand-up comedy started (Macdonald, 2016).

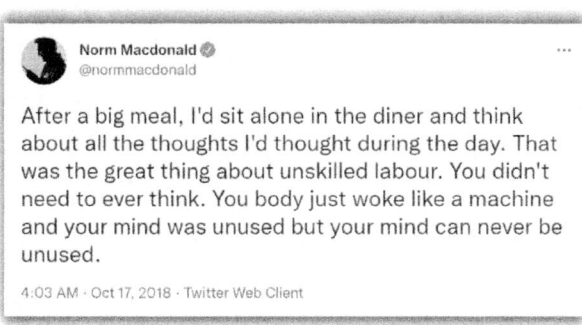

Norm Macdonald ✔
@normmacdonald

After a big meal, I'd sit alone in the diner and think about all the thoughts I'd thought during the day. That was the great thing about unskilled labour. You didn't need to ever think. You body just woke like a machine and your mind was unused but your mind can never be unused.

4:03 AM · Oct 17, 2018 · Twitter Web Client

Quick Ascent to Stardom

When Macdonald did venture into stand-up comedy, his initial rise to stardom happened relatively quickly. He quickly rose to the top of the Canadian stand-up circuit, and moving to L.A. at the age of 31, his unique comic style and persona caught the eyes and ears of Dennis Miller, then hot from his SNL *Weekend Update* stint and having just started *The Dennis Miller Show* on HBO. Team Miller sent Macdonald a communique on whether he might be interested in writing for Miller's new show and requested that Macdonald send in a package of material for consideration. Macdonald struggled to write ten jokes, and because he felt that nine of them were subpar, he submitted only what he thought was the one good joke of the bunch. Miller took this as "some kind of (Andy) Kaufman move" and hired Macdonald as a result. After working for Miller, Macdonald would then become a writer for the *Roseanne* sitcom.

But it was as the irreverent host of SNL's *Weekend Update* from 1994 through 1998 that Macdonald shot to cultural stardom. With his acerbic wit, deadpan delivery, and a mischievous gleam in his eye, he brought an edge and hint of subversion to the longstanding 'fake news' SNL segment.

Behind a Midwesterner-via-Canada demeanor of folksy charm and affability, Macdonald would read obscure news stories with the punchline, so to speak, oftentimes being a non sequitur or coming in the form of him articulating a "note to self" into his mini cassette recorder.[8] He'd savage pop culture figures of the time, with Michael Jackson and O.J. Simpson among his favorite targets. "The nation is still reeling from Thursday's bombshell announcement that Lisa Marie Presley has filed for divorce from Michael Jackson," Macdonald quipped from behind the desk, "According to friends, the two

were never a good match. She's more of a stay-at-home type, and he's more of a homosexual pedophile." His O.J. jokes were legion; after Simpson's not-guilty verdict was rendered, Macdonald wryly noted (in something that is not so much a joke as a dark satirical condemnation): "Well, it is finally official: Murder is legal in the state of California."

When NBC executive Don Ohlmeyer, a golfing buddy of O.J.'s, sent word that he wanted Macdonald to tone down the O.J. jokes, Macdonald did the exact opposite: he dialed his anti-O.J. crusade up to eleven, which eventually cost him his coveted job at SNL (though in later years, he would downplay Ohlmeyer's O.J. connection as the reason he was fired)[9].

---

[8] In *Based on a True Story* (2016), Macdonald credits the "note to self" gag to *Weekend Update* writer Frank Sebastiano, which he reiterates in Matthews (2016).

[9] In his January 7, 1998 appearance on David Letterman's show (https://youtu.be/tudRJETrphxk), Macdonald indirectly makes the Ohlmeyer-O.J. connection and indirectly assigns blame to Ohlmeyer. However, in his 2011 interview with Marc Maron, Macdonald says he doesn't necessarily believe Ohlmeyer fired him for his O.J. jokes, and that it could have been a decision made lower on the food chain, noting that during his *Weekend Update* stint he was not a team player with the rest of the cast, which upset many, possibly even Lorne Michaels himself (Maron, 2011). Jim Downey, Macdonald's writing partner on *Weekend Update*, notes: "I'm not sure how big a fan Lorne was of our *Update*. I think it was probably too mean for his sensibility, and he didn't like the deadpan aspect of it. But he supported us as long as he could, bless his heart" (Sacks, 2014).

After leaving SNL, huge breakthrough post-SNL success (of the sort that, for example, Adam Sandler, Mike Myers, or Will Ferrell have experienced) eluded him, and the Hollywood aspect of Macdonald's career was uneven at best. His movie *Dirty Work* (1998), which bombed at the box office, has since developed a cult following. *Screwed* (2000), his next and final movie as a leading-man, was so disastrous that most people don't even know it exists.

From 1999 to 2001, Macdonald had his own ABC sitcom *The Norm Show*, a conventional, laugh-track based sitcom of the sort that almost every successful stand-up comedian had at the time, but which Macdonald hated making.[10] Then there was a series of false starts or cancelled-early shows, including a 2003 Fox sitcom called *A Minute with Stan Hooper* (cancelled after just six episodes); *Back to Norm* (2005), a forced and largely unfunny sketch show on Comedy Central that didn't get past pilot stage; and the funny but short-lived *Sports Show with Norm Macdonald* (2011) on Comedy Central. In 2006, he released *Ridiculous*, a sketch comedy album (titled after one of his favorite words).

Between 2013 and 2018 he did his well-received podcast *Norm Macdonald Live*, wrote his very funny semi-fictional memoir *Based on a True Story* (2016), did a string of absurdist KFC ads as a Colonel Sanders imposter, and then hosted a no frills, very loose Netflix anti-talkshow-talkshow called *Norm Macdonald Has a Show* (2018). In between, he did voiceover work for animated movies and television shows, and had many cameos in various movies and sitcoms. "I can see that my life since SNL has been a full sprint, with all my might to outrun the wolves of irrelevancy snapping at my heels," he writes in *Based on a True Story*.

Finding a proper and fitting mass media vehicle for his unique talents proved difficult. He dreamed of being a late night talk show host. But apart from his stand-up, the ideal venue for Macdonald may have been less as an interviewer than as an interviewee. It is significant that the most popular video clips of Macdonald, which have led many a Norm fan down hours of YouTube rabbit holes, involve him as a talk show guest, reading the room, and telling long jokes or reacting to questions with his improvisational skills.

Throughout his career, he would state how much he enjoyed the process of writing stand-up material (e.g., Brownstein 1991), and he'd

---

[10] See Wild (1999).

spend the bulk of his professional time as a hardened, night club road warrior, doing a huge number of shows each year on the stand-up circuit. It was on the stage (he preferred small rooms to large venues) where he felt most comfortable, interacting with his audience and shaping his material.

Norm Being Norm

A very private and reclusive person, when not on the road doing stand-up Macdonald, an avid reader, rarely left his condominium. He could be described as a fabulist, prone to making up stories about himself. In his particular case, the evasiveness was designed to mislead people from knowing too much about his past, particularly the cancer experiences he'd had since his youth, and towards crafting his comedic persona as a 'dumb guy'. He would repeatedly intimate that he'd dropped out of high school, when (as noted earlier) he actually graduated high school at age 14. He would say he grew up very poor on a failed farm, when in actuality both of his parents were teachers, his father eventually becoming a school vice-principal (Neil Macdonald, 2016).[11]

Macdonald's DGAF ethos was commensurate with his private life. He was a man of few possessions, which he felt weighs one down, and in his last years lived in a modest two-bedroom condominium nearly devoid of furnishings.

Various interviews reveal some of Macdonald's psychological idiosyncrasies. He was an admitted hypochondriac (understandable given his lifelong struggle with cancer) and would get panic attacks of the sort where he literally felt like he was going to die.[12] He noted that he had Stendhal Syndrome, a type of panic attack that occurs after being overwhelmed by what the subject perceives as great beauty (Maron, 2011). He admitted to being an obsessive compulsive, and of course there was his chronic gambling addiction. In a variety of different contexts, including about the intense stage fright he

---

[11] See also Munroe (2016). Macdonald also makes these "I grew up poor" claims in *Based on a True Story*. One profile of Macdonald states that his farm experience consisted of summers at a grandparents' farm near Avonmore, Ontario (Giovannone, 2021), which would be commensurate with both of his parents having summers off as teachers. See also Standard-Freeholder (2021).

[12] *Larry King Now*, August 3, 2015, https://youtu.be/gKkWVK2N4VU.

would get, Macdonald would cite his use of Xanax. He'd often say he doesn't drink or do drugs, but there were periods of his life when he did drink.

He has stated he saw a psychiatrist four times as a child, and that as an adult he saw a Fifth Avenue psychiatrist to address his gambling addiction.[13] In 2009, when asked by a morning radio DJ whether he sees a therapist, Macdonald said that he doesn't believe in psychotherapy and disagrees with their approaches. In the same interview, he later adds: "The problem with antidepressants is then you don't face life. I mean, why not just do heroin?"[14]

He was likely a savant to some degree. For instance, despite his intellectual interests and comedic brilliance, he never learned to drive. Geoff Edgers, the reporter who got closest to Macdonald, notes that "sometimes he has problems with basic sorts of tasks," adding that while accompanying Macdonald to NBC Studios in New York City for an appearance on *The Tonight Show Starring Jimmy Fallon*, Macdonald loses the sheet of paper that had the jokes he wanted to tell, and then later loses his wallet – which is eventually found by Lori Jo Hoekstra, who in addition to being his longtime producing partner and friend served in many ways as his minder (Edgers, WBUR, 2021).

At one point during his guest appearance on *Norm Macdonald Live*, David Letterman says to him: "We always worry a little about you because we regard you as the top of the heap, the best of the best, the funniest of the funny, the guy who has it in every fiber of his being, not conjured, the real thing."[15]

Macdonald was once-married, in 1988, having a son named Dylan (whom he named after Dylan Thomas) and whom he often expressed his deep love for, but was divorced in 1999. He never dated again, often joking about how clumsy and awkward he is with women, and later embracing a relatively ascetic lifestyle as a rational (albeit admittedly futile) form of resistance against the existential dread of death's inevitability. While it's difficult to listen to (due to the two super-annoying and vacuous radio personalities), the pair of morning

---

[13] *Norm Macdonald Live*, July 25, 2017, https://vimeo.com/455414036. From his retelling, it sounds like the Fifth Avenue treatments were reluctantly attended by him, and were most likely arranged during his time at *Saturday Night Live*.

[14] *The Sarah & Vinnie Show*, Interview with Norm Macdonald, August 31, 2009, https://youtu.be/zSQj2HIpA7Y?t=2771. It's unclear how Macdonald squared his characterization of antidepressants with his presumed use of Xanax.

[15] *Norm Macdonald Live*, July 25, 2017, https://vimeo.com/455414036.

radio interviews Macdonald did on *The Sarah & Vinnie Show* (in 2008 & 2009) highlights the profound contrast between his austere and ascetic lifestyle versus the two grating radio interviewers who one could say represent the more debased and decadent elements of the contemporary neoliberal culture industry.[16]

In one of these interviews, when pressed about his dating life, Macdonald replies that he does not date, does not visit prostitutes, and has not had sex in 10 years (which would be around the time of his divorce). "I find sex very repetitive and dull and kind of pointless," he says. He notes that he did have "lots of sex" when he was a young man, but now finds it a childish desire which he's spiritually outgrown. Both his deep Christianity and his particular strain of existential fatalism seem to have been the driving factors of the 'incel' sexual abstinence he adhered to since his divorce. "I find sex to be a very filthy act," he says in the interview, "in the sense of being shameful," arguing that sex is an activity we don't do in public due to its intrinsic shamefulness. "As the scriptures say," he begins to tell the deejays, "when you're a boy you do a boy's things, and when you're a man you… [*Interrupted by deejays*]… I know most people are children for their whole life and it's a way of having fun." When asked if he has a best friend he can go to when he's down, to talk things out with, he says he doesn't do that anymore. It's one of the darkest sentiments Macdonald ever expressed:

> "I used to do that stuff. I came to the realization that we're all plunging headlong into death… So, to me, if you're plunging down an abyss, headlong into death, the idea of grabbing onto another human being just to touch them for a moment on your way seems futile to me. It seems more pathetic than facing it, just to me personally. I don't condemn people for doing that. I try to look at life square in the eye, as terrifying as it is, and it is the most terrifying thing there is. Because being alive means dying."

Macdonald's perspective on 'success' in the entertainment industry, while prescient, was also reflective of his stoic attitude:

---

[16] *The Sarah & Vinnie Show,* Interviews with Norm Macdonald (September 23, 2008 & August 31, 2009), https://www.youtube.com/watch?v=zSQj2HIpA7Y

"You can be a failure by the world's standards and still feel lucky. There are so many different ways of grading failure and success. When you hit a certain point of success, or even geographically, being in Hollywood, for instance, you're surrounded by so much incredible success that it's easy to feel like a failure. Even though you feel like an asshole trying to explain it." (Matthews, 2016).

His career seemed to hop from one life raft to another. Other than the stand-up stage, there was no easy fit for 'Normism' in the Hollywood entertainment industry. Of Macdonald's career, SNL founder Lorne Michaels draws a comparison to Don Rickles, noting that Rickles' style of humor was not to everyone's taste, and then adding: "Whenever I've seen Norm live in any kind of performance situation, he's brilliant. We talk about wishing more people knew Norm and that he had more commercial success. Is he perhaps not meant for that?" (Edgers, 2016).

Macdonald never seemed to have much of a plan and there was "a fog of dysfunction surrounding him" (Edgers, 2021). In a 2019 conversation, both Conan O'Brien and David Letterman agree that Macdonald may not be the hardest working comedian in show business, but that his persona, combined with the caliber of his material and delivery, put him at the same level as someone (such as Steve Martin) who works extremely hard on their act.[17] Apathy, or stoic disregard or some combination of both, did seem to be a Macdonald trait, perhaps serving as a coping mechanism for what may have been, despite his assertions to the contrary, his depressive qualities.[18] One exception to Macdonald's apathy took place in 2014, when he lobbied publicly and earnestly to be given a late-night talk show on CBS, after Craig Ferguson announced he was exiting *The Late Late Show* (Marchese, 2014). Macdonald would later learn that, unbeknownst to him, David Letterman had lobbied hard for him to get the job, but failed. CBS opted instead for James Corden.

---

[17] *Conan O'Brien Needs a Friend*, Interview with David Letterman, October 7, 2019, https://podcasts.apple.com/us/podcast/40-david-letterman/id1438054347?i=1000452586161.

[18] "I'm not depressed at all. I'm in no ways depressed," he said in a 2009 radio interview (*The Sarah & Vinnie Show*, Interview with Norm Macdonald, August 31, 2009, https://youtu.be/zSQj2HIpA7Y?t=2810).

In 2015, when asked if he thinks radio is a better medium for imaginative comedy, Macdonald replied: "I like radio comedy, which doesn't exist anymore. I was thinking of doing an old-timey radio [podcast] thing," and then explains how, because one cannot see the subjects on a radio program, a certain descriptor, when revealed (for example, the color of a person's shirt), "works *after* the joke that you just heard, informs the joke afterwards."[19]

Part of Macdonald's 'failure to launch' was likely due to his aversion to the hierarchical social dynamics involved. "I don't like powerful people. I don't like power. I don't like people that have power over me. I don't like to have power over anyone else. It's my least favorite thing in life… having to answer to anybody, or expecting anyone to answer to me. Man, I hate that" (MacPherson, 2012).

His professional integrity, though, combined with what he acknowledged as luck, kept him afloat:

> "Fortunately, I don't really care about success or money or shit. I could give a f*ck. I hate fame. I hate being recognized, because I don't know how to talk to people... I don't have any ambition. [Laughs.] I got my computer. The great thing about the computer is that you only need enough money to buy a computer and some food, and you're all right. I don't have to go to premières. I don't have to go to people's f*cking parties. I don't have to meet actors. I'm really blessed that I don't have to do all that horseshit" (Heisler, 2011).

There was certainly something of a loner quality in him, which can be gleaned from not only his writings, interviews, and stand-up performances, but from his other friends from the SNL world (e.g., Dennis Miller, David Spade), many of whom have relayed stories of his quirky habit of being ridiculously late or not showing up at all.[20] He "spends a lot of time alone," notes Geoff Edgers (WBUR, 2021). In his very insightful 2016 *Washington Post* profile of Macdonald, Edgers writes: "He is not anti-social so much as socially reluctant. In an industry centered around parties and red carpets, he prefers the

---

[19] CBC, "Norm Macdonald in Studio Q", February 2, 2015, https://youtu.be/wxuFAeOe4FI?t=209.

[20] https://youtu.be/7Fh30X1Zgf0

privacy of his home or, after a gig, clicking through the channels in his hotel room" (Edgers, 2016). The short 5 minute video that accompanies Edgers' piece, where he is interviewing Macdonald in his modest condo unit, is a fascinating glimpse into how frugal and pedestrian Macdonald's home life was.[21]

Dan Brooks provides a good synopsis of a typical day for Macdonald:

> Macdonald is a creature of habit, and many of those habits are not conducive to the advancement of his career. He doesn't go to parties. He doesn't schmooze. He doesn't drive, which in Los Angeles is like being confined to an iron lung. He used to live in West Hollywood, which made it easy to drop by the Comedy Store for surprise sets. But now he lives in a planned community with his adult son, Dylan, next to the home he bought for his mother. He's deep in the wad of office parks and car dealerships near LAX and has to take a hundred-dollar Uber to get to the Comedy Store, so he rarely does. By his own admission, he spends a lot of time at home, going down what he calls "rabbit holes" on YouTube or watching sports on television. The night before our dinner, he stayed up until dawn live-tweeting the World Series of Poker (Brooks, 2018).

---

[21] https://www.dailymotion.com/video/x3rjszt

Gambling

Macdonald was a sports fanatic, and his notorious gambling addiction – from sports betting to card playing -- is legendary. He freely admitted to it, and stated in several different interviews that he lost his entire fortune three times to gambling, with the largest amount lost on a single bet (a football game) being $400,000 (Maron, 2011).[22] In his sketch album *Ridiculous* (2006), three separate but connected bits (Gambling Sportscaster", "Half-Time", and "Two-Minute Warning") revolve around a gambling-addicted TV football color commentator whose entire commentary pivots around the specifics of beating the game's spread.

When asked what it is like to lose everything, he assumed a Buddhist tone, framing the experience as ultimately a positive thing:

> "Well, oddly enough, it feels kind of good. You know, you just go to the coffee shop, you sit there, and you feel clean of everything. Of course, when you lose it all, it's a tremendous body blow at first. But you see it coming for a while before you realize you're out of control. And afterwards, I don't know, there's something nice about having nothing. I mean, if you have enough to eat, and about ten feet or so to lie in, then in truth that's all you need. Everything else you just buy, and then eventually don't like, and then find in your closet later and go, 'Why did I get this?' (Gheciu, 2016).

He tried to make sense of what underlay his attraction to gambling, to put it into some sort of context, and once described the activity of gambling as a state of being where "what you're addicted to is hope… When the dice are in the air, anything can happen."[23] One can see his penchant for gambling as representative of the certain existentialist strain in his overall approach to both comedy and life itself. This is directly addressed in *Based on a True Story*, where he describes in more detail gambling as an intense rush of hope that occurs after the throw of the dice but before the landing:

---

[22] See also Schudel (2021). For a firsthand account of Macdonald's compulsive gambling behavior, see Kaplan (2021).

[23] https://youtu.be/wMjHd6fyX3k

I remember a psychiatrist once telling me that I gamble in order to escape the reality of life, and I told him that's why everyone does everything. But I've had plenty of wasted nights, after losses and bigger losses, to consider the question more seriously. So why the attraction? Most people would think it's the wins that keep the gambler going, but any gambler knows this is not true. As you place your chips on the craps table, you feel anxiety and impatience. When the red dice hit the green felt with a thunk and you're declared the winner and the chips are pushed toward you, you feel relief. Relief is all. And relief is fine, but hardly what a man would give the whole rest of his life to gain. It has to be something else, and the best I've come up with is this: It is a particular moment. A magic moment that occurs after the placing of a bet and before the result of that bet. It is after the red dice are thrown but before they lie still on the green felt where they fall. It is when the dice are in the air, and as long as they are there, time stops. As long as the red dice are in the air, the gambler has hope. And hope is a wonderful thing to be addicted to.

Elsewhere in the book, a fictional life-or-death bet is depicted in a passage intended to elicit the allure of gambling:

I feel great excitement at what lies ahead. The enormity of the stakes, the idea of a game being played for life and death, does not sober me but instead does the opposite. I feel drunk with confidence. A simple piece of logic convinces me I will win. I cannot conceive of my own death, and since a loss would result in such, it follows that I cannot conceive of my own loss.

Later, towards the end of the book, he writes:

And as for my gambling, it's true I lost it all a few times. But that's because I always took the long shot and it never came in. But I still have some time before I cross that river. And if you're at the table and you're rolling them bones, then there's no money in playing it safe. You have to take all your chips and put them on double six and watch as every eye goes to

15

you and then to those red dice doing their wild dance and freezing time before finding the cruel green felt.

While Macdonald's life-long gambling addiction was well known, what was not well-known was that he was an avid reader with a wide array of philosophical interests, which he increasingly wove into his comedy.

TWO

Comedic Style

The Comedian's Comedian

Long known as a comedian's comedian, with a cult following of dedicated fans, one can peruse YouTube to see virtually every established comic today referring to Macdonald as the gold standard and among the greatest ever, certainly among the best – if not *the* best – during his time as a performer. (Most everyone refers to him as just "Norm" and in stand-up comedy circles, "Norm" unmistakably refers to just one individual). He never experienced the huge, breakout success other comedians have had and never put much value in pursuing it, but as an iconoclastic comic voice his influence within the world of comedy far outstrips any commercial appeal he may have had.

You either got Norm Macdonald or you didn't.[24] His style could be meandering, but when it came to punchlines his rhythm and timing were impeccable. Behind an ever-present Cheshire Cat grin, the minutest changes in his tone, cadence, and inflection provided the unique stamp that was 'Norm', the envy of many other successful stand-up comedians. His style of speaking, Canadian and provincial, and his use of unusual euphemisms, made him sound like he was from another era. A discussion between Conan O'Brien, Andy Richter, and their longtime show producer Frank Smiley, which occurred shortly after Macdonald's passing, is a particularly incisive

---

[24] Someone who doesn't get Macdonald is Malcolm Gladwell, who writes: "I never found him funny at all… There's another 'famous' Norm Macdonald appearance on Conan, in which Macdonald tells an excruciatingly long joke about a moth. Kind of. But comedy insiders love it, because if you've actually done comedy, and realize how fragile the relationship between comic and audience is, you realize just how much chutzpah it takes to launch into a story with an impossibly distant punch line. The insider watches that, and says — *how on earth did he pull that off?* The outsider changes channels" (Gladwell, 2021).

17

and moving testament to Macdonald's originality, comedic inscrutability, and willingness to cross PC boundaries.[25]

"Even when Macdonald's comedy ventured into the offensive," one writer notes, "he performed it with an almost childlike innocence that dulled the edginess and revealed the inherent absurdity of whatever he was joking about" (Andrelczyk, 2021). Another writer aptly describes Macdonald's act as "sunny nihilism" (Parker, 2016); yet another refers to Macdonald as a "Zen provocateur" (Harvilla, 2021). Through a very stylized delivery, much of his material on the follies and foibles of the human condition did contain a Buddhist-like outlook (although, given his ascetic lifestyle and religious beliefs, a Christian monk's outlook is equally apropos), and from a certain angle Macdonald's beaming smile and entire way-of-being resembled a pop-culture rendition of the Buddha (albeit one with a dark streak of existential angst). This description is more fitting for his later years, when he dropped much of the hard cynicism of his earlier years and pivoted towards more earnest comedy and conversations dealing with themes of love and death.[26] With later Macdonald, the joke was like a Zen koan. There was also something of the trickster in him, particularly in his more experimental projects (e.g., *Based on a True Story*; *Norm Macdonald has a Show*).

The snappy and necessary abrupt pace of his *Weekend Update* format gained a dedicated following, largely due to Macdonald's style, how he'd lean-in while delivering a punchline, hang onto a joke, and stare into the camera with a smirk for unusually long beats. Jim Downey, the longtime SNL writer who was Macdonald's primary writing partner during his *Weekend Update* years, noted the punk attitude of their venture together: "What I did like about the way we approached *Update* was that it was akin to what the punk movement was for music… We weren't going to be easy… We were going to be mean and, to an extent, anarchists" (Sacks, 2014).

Macdonald's style would in later years transition towards a more folksy and relaxed delivery, peppered with unusual words and turns

---

[25] *Conan O'Brien Needs a Friend*, September 16, 2021,
https://omny.fm/shows/conan-o-brien-needs-a-friend/conan-talks-about-norm-macdonald.

[26] Macdonald credits Sam Kinison, who mentored him while Macdonald opened for him during a Canadian stand-up tour, with advising him to do comedy on topics he cares about, instead of "just cats and dogs" (Macpherson, 2012).

of phrase. He attributes this aspect of his joke-telling style to growing up around old men:

> "My father had me when he was 58. He went through the Depression and all this stuff, and all of his friends were old men. When I was young, I was steeped in this. I really liked old men and how they spoke, and I thought it was really funny how they told stories and the words they used, and I absorbed all that. Ever since I started doing comedy, I would use more old words and literate words and I found that mixing the two would create a very good comedy quiver" (Rose, 2021).

Influences

Among his favorite stand-up comedians, he frequently cited Bob Hope, Don Rickles, and Rodney Dangerfield, but as his own stand-up career matured, Macdonald began to adopt a style more reminiscent of Richard Pryor, also one of his comedy heroes.[27] He began to consciously build his act from a foundation of inversion, which in time coalesced into the 'Normness' imprint by which he is most fondly remembered: the 'dumb guy' talking about 'smart things', such as the existential mysteries found in the dark corners of the human condition. The awareness with which he tailored both his material and his delivery to this public persona is evident in many of his interviews:

> "Steve Martin told me when he started out he was dressed as a hippie, and that shocked me. He was like, 'Well, I was doing avant-garde stuff. Then suddenly I realized avant-garde comes out better from a guy in a white suit.' I thought that's pretty f*cking smart" (Marchese, 2014).

In describing what makes good comedy, he says: "It's not just the truth in what you say, but in the persona the audience sees performing. You have to learn who you are" (Munroe, 2016). Elsewhere, Macdonald has described his approach to comedy as a

---

[27] See Rytlewski (2009).

thematic inversion of Jerry Seinfeld's formula. When asked why the subject of death often appears in his material, Macdonald reveals this key dynamic of his style:

> "When I started comedy, I really admired guys like Seinfeld, who will take little things and get very upset about them, like a Corn Flakes box or something. But I realized, that's what makes it work: He puts such importance into such a trivial matter, that's such a funny way to do it. And then I wondered if the flip could work, because I'm always trying to see the other way to do it. I started wondering if I could talk about very big issues in a very off-handed, trivial way" (Rose, 2021).

In a 2012 interview, Macdonald's analysis of Bob Hope is highly instructive in revealing the style of comedy he holds in the highest regard and for also revealing how Macdonald's knowledge of comedic form and presentation – the mechanics of comedy – consciously shaped his own comedic style. "The only virtue in comedy is to be funny," Macdonald says. While he expresses admiration for Richard Pryor's completely different style of stand-up, his personal ideal is someone like Bob Hope:

> "Bob Hope is a fantastic comic because he never went serious… There's two types of guys [in comedy]. There's guys like Pryor, who are brilliant because they're so vulnerable and you know who they are, and then there's guys like Bob Hope who are brilliant because they're like invisible. To me, Bob Hope in a way is a little bit on a higher level because he presents a sort of existential view of life, where everything is reduced to the breeziest jokes possible. It doesn't even seem like he's a person. It seems like he's a cartoon. And I think if you can rise to the level of cartoon… because he's funnier than like Bugs Bunny" (MacPherson, 2012).

With regard to the fact that Bob Hope used an army of joke writers, Macdonald observes that while there are no Bob Hope jokes that everyone remembers (and that Hope's jokes weren't all that good), he still made us smile, which is a testament to his skills as a stand-up comic, "because he didn't need jokes". Macdonald then makes a very specific observation about Hope's style of delivery that anticipates Macdonald's own lean-in-and-stare-down-the-audience style of punchline delivery:

> "Hope did a very specific thing… He would do the joke, then they would cut to close-up on him and he would look into the audience. He would put a flash of fear into his eyes as if he had just been caught, like he was an imposter, like he knew the joke was bad and the jig was up… It was a very subtle, quick-fast thing, but *that's* what made everyone laugh. They didn't know why they were laughing. But *that's* why they were laughing. I know, because I've watched it so many times" (MacPherson, 2012).

Macdonald then references a major turning point in his own understanding of comedy, something he would increasingly try to incorporate into his act:

> "I've come to this thing… I realize that there's laughter and then there's smiling. And I think that in the end – I've only come to this realization in the last couple of years in comedy, because I always wanted to punch people in the stomach and make them laugh so hard they couldn't stop – but I've come to understand that just smiling and the spread of goodwill might be a higher art form than really heavy, hard laughter" (MacPherson, 2012).

In addition to Hope, Macdonald cites Bill Cosby and Charlie Chaplin as examples of this unique and higher comedic form. "Whenever I think of Chaplin, I smile more than I laugh out loud." The way such performers embody, and are at one with, their material is what Macdonald admires about them. "It's probably a gift that you either have or you don't."[28]

---

[28] In this same interview, Macdonald juxtaposes the comedic form of these figures against someone like George Carlin. "As brilliant as Carlin was," Macdonald observes, "he didn't make you happy".

The DGAF Mark Twain

In many ways, Macdonald came off as something of a modern-day Mark Twain, with dashes of Andy Kaufman's unpredictability and willingness to frustrate the audience. In his Foreword to *Based on a True Story*, comedian Louis C.K., a good friend and admirer of Macdonald's, writes:

> "I have been a student of comedy my whole life and I honestly don't know how he does any of it… A lot of comics over the years have been compared to Mark Twain, but I think Norm is the only one who actually matches the guy in terms of his voice and ability… He falls into no genre or category. Just comedian."

A true DGAF artist, Macdonald neither pandered, compromised, nor craved approval. He had no publicist (similar to how fellow Zen provocateur Bill Murray has no manager or agent). He never donned typical stand-up comedian attire, be it the suit & tie look or the jeans & t-shirt look, but wore whatever he happened to be wearing that day. (He once co-hosted an outdoor red-carpet event wearing sweatpants). He admired how Dean Martin, when doing his own variety show later in his career, "didn't care" and would wing it in sketches with drink and cigarette in hand, essentially playing a version of himself in every sketch (*Playboy*, 1997).[29] "Maybe Macdonald really is just in it for the jokes and the admiration of his peers," reads one profile of him, "and what looks by other standards like a series of disappointments is, to him, success enough" (Brooks, 2018). Steve Higgins, the very funny former SNL writer and announcer/sidekick on *The Tonight Show Starring Jimmy Fallon* describes Macdonald's comedic form as "that kind of comedy where it's deconstructed and served back to you… It also may be the reason he's not giant. Because maybe he's too funny." (Edgers, 2016) Similarly, after Macdonald's passing, Dave Foley tweeted: "I thought he was way too funny to be successful. I was half right."[30]

Despite the deep humility he showed on most fronts, Macdonald knew that, as a comedian, he was good. His love and respect for the

---

[29] See also Gordon (2017).
[30] https://twitter.com/DaveSFoley/status/1437862694103629825

aesthetic form of quality comedy, as well as where he thought the form could go, meant that he consciously strove for innovation towards this purity of form, and refrained from the compromises that would come if he strove for mass appeal:

> "[Because] I can do stand-up at such a high level, I can do any type of comedy. I can do the hardest things. I mean, the book was incredibly challenging, and I did that. But I know I'm a niche comedian. I'll never be [a] fully mainstream comedian, although I've thought of trying to do that... *Why don't I just be Bob Hope? That would be fun.* I could've made even more people happy by doing that, but I decided to go a way that I knew wouldn't be as lucrative or successful. And mostly I'm glad I did" (Marchese, 2016).[31]

Macdonald frequently noted that he's happiest, and most professionally satisfied, when doing stand-up before an audience, once saying: "I'm no good at anything but comedy, which I think I'm good at. I'm absolutely no good at networking; I'm terrible at acting; I'm terrible at dealing with executives; I'm terrible at collaborating. And I say whatever I want to say. But I think I'm good enough at comedy that I can survive. And I don't really have an ambition for money."[32] He has noted how, in his early years of stand-up, he'd simply do his jokes, and was afraid of interacting with the audience, also thinking it hackneyed at the time (Gordon, 2017). But as he grew older and matured as a stand-up performer, he came to realize that the audience loves interaction, as it personalizes the experience. He also came to largely abandon honing down an act and repeating it night after night. "I would feel so embarrassed doing the same act twice, even in the same night. At one point, I took a year off to come up with five different shows, so I would have a different show every night at the same club" (Brownstein, 2021).

---

[31] In 2009, he told an interviewer: "Listen, I'll do any f*cking other thing, other than stand-up, for money. Like, I'll do the worst movie, the worst TV show; I don't give a f*cking sh*t about that stuff. But stand-up, I've got to go with merit on that one. I mean, I don't like being immodest, but in this one particular area I don't want anybody else's hands touching it. I mean, I'm a whore like everybody else, because I take money from things I'm no good at, but the stand-up itself, I want merit more than success" (Rytlewski, 2009).

[32] https://www.brainyquote.com/quotes/norm_macdonald_557253

Meta-Comedy

Macdonald's comedic style exudes an aloofness and childlike bewilderment that hides his comic precision. In his pursuit of the pure joke, in his attempt to pare it down to its essence, he crafted his material in an almost Wittgensteinian fashion. Over the years, the more thoughtful profiles of him have pointed to the contours and qualities of his comedic style. "At a moment when comedians work for applause as much as laughter, by being vulnerable, honest, outspoken, socially relevant," writes Dan Brooks, "Macdonald is still pursuing the laugh — and nothing more. This anachronistic approach might be limiting his audience, but it could also explain his enduring appeal, because it lends him a kind of moral authority. He is something like a comedy ascetic, demanding a purity that temporal jokes cannot achieve…" (Brooks, 2018). In describing Macdonald's style, Andrew Chow writes: "Macdonald thrived on the edge of convention and in moments of silence and discomfort; through his unique approach, he weaved the dumbest punchlines into comedic masterclasses. And while other comics turned their desire to provoke into an excuse to bully or punch down, Macdonald's transgressions were usually more conceptual: he thumbed his nose at the art form of the joke itself" (Chow, 2021). "As off-kilter and off-the-cuff as his comedy can seem," writes Dave Itzkoff, "Mr. Macdonald has always sought precise control of it. At *Weekend Update*, he said he was 'doing a specific experiment, where I was trying to strip all cleverness from the joke and try and make it as blunt as possible.' He added, 'I always told everybody the perfect joke would be where the setup and punch line were identical'" (Itzkoff, 2011). Macdonald believed the closest he came to this was a *Weekend Update* joke from 1995 about the divorce of Julia Roberts (then at her hottest) and Lyle Lovett (who was never hot). "Julia Roberts told reporters this week that her marriage to Lyle Lovett has been over for some time," Macdonald deadpans, "The key moment, she said, came when she realized that she was Julia Roberts, and that she was married to Lyle Lovett."

With respect to whether or not his material could be deemed 'subversive', Macdonald observed that stand-up comedy "is a form and to subvert something, you have to do it perfectly first… You just want little drops of subversion. Letterman in the '80s would be 90 percent a great talk show and then 10 percent subversion. If you get to 30 percent subversion, you're in Andy Kaufman land. If you get to 70 percent, you're a guy on the streets screaming at people" (Marchese, 2018).

A joke's effectiveness is often a function of the linguistic incongruity relative to the multiple meanings a word can possess, and Macdonald was quite unique in his idealizing of, in an almost Platonic way, the pure form of a joke, stripping it of artifice, toying with its structure, deconstructing its constituent elements, and then creatively restructuring the ways in which, for example, a simple pun or non-sequitur can operate. One might describe his style as high-concept comedy, sometimes bordering on performance art. He was very much concerned with the authenticity of comedy material. He disliked the term 'anti-comedy' being used to describe him, and perhaps a more fitting description would be 'meta-comedy' (although he's disparaged that term also).[33]

Embracing the Bomb

If an audience didn't react to one his jokes, rather than quickly moving on to something else as most other comedians would normally do, Macdonald would instead commit to the bomb, let it linger, and then double-down with further ad-libbed comments upon (or elucidations of) the joke itself. "There's a difference between a clap and a laugh," Macdonald has stated. "A laugh is involuntary, but the crowd is in complete control when they're clapping. They're saying, 'We agree with what you're saying; proceed!' But when they're laughing, they're genuinely surprised. And when they're not laughing, they're *really* surprised. And sometimes I think, in my little head, that that's the best comedy of all" (Rytlewski, 2009). It was at the outer edges of this perspective and practice that Macdonald would sometimes exhibit Kaufman-esque mischievousness towards the audience. "I don't know why, but to me the funniest thing is trying to

---

[33] Macdonald did only a couple of stand-up specials, and didn't particularly like the format, as it forced him to hone an act for posterity, and didn't allow him to riff as freely as he normally would at a routine stand-up performance. See Rytlewski (2009). Avoid (or take with a grain of salt) Comedy Central's *Norm Macdonald: Me Doing Stand-Up* (2011) unless it's the completely uncut and uncensored audio version; otherwise, the commercial-breaks completely interrupt the flow of the material. Far better is Netflix's *Hitler's Dog, Gossip & Trickery* (2017); there is no censoring, no commercials, and the late-stage Macdonald material is better.

make people laugh and having them hate you. If you're a bad singer, they feel sorry for you. But if you're trying to make them laugh and you fail, they hate you so bad. Whenever I would bomb, I'd get happy. Comedy is about unexpected things. So if you're trying to make a guy laugh and he doesn't, that's funny, right?" (*Playboy*, 1997).

An example of this is Macdonald's oft-cited contribution to Comedy Central's 2008 Roast of Bob Saget. A close and longtime friend of Saget's, Macdonald did not want to participate, as he was not a fan of the personal viciousness characteristic of celebrity roasts, but relented after Saget pleaded with him to participate. The show's producers encouraged Macdonald to be dirty and raunchy, and Macdonald gave all the signals that he would do so, but when it came his turn at the microphone, he turned his roasting of Saget into a conceptual piece by deliberately going soft, delivering clean and corny jokes from a 1940s joke book, much to the audience's consternation but to the other roasters' delight. He ends his short routine with some heartfelt words praising Saget's kindness.

Later in the Saget roast is a fantastic moment that distills Macdonald's essence. At such events, comedians usually throw barbs not only at the guest of honor but also at the other personalities doing the night's roasting. During comedian Jim Norton's turn at the microphone, he turns to Macdonald and says: "Norm Macdonald, God bless you. Watching your set was like watching Henry Fonda pick blueberries." The audience laughs. Several extended beats into the crowd's laughter, Macdonald, with a bemused smile and a quizzical look, delivers a comeback with perfect aplomb: "Why, I don't think there's a person in here that would not *love* to watch Henry Fonda pick blueberries." The audience cheers, Norton himself laughs, and Macdonald prevails.

THREE

A Favorite Late Night Guest

It was the meta-aspect of Macdonald's act that made him a favorite guest on late night talk shows, especially the shows of David Letterman and Conan O'Brien, both of whom tirelessly championed Macdonald. "If we could have, we would have had Norm on every damn week," Letterman says. "He is funny in a way that some people inhale and exhale. With others, you can tell the comedy, the humor is considered. With Norm, he exudes it. It's sort of a furnace in him because he's so effortless. The combination of the delivery and his appearance and his intelligence. There may be people as funny as Norm, but I don't know anybody who is funnier" (Edgers, 2016). Conan O'Brien observes "Part of what makes him so compelling and so fun to watch is that he defies categorization" (Edgers, 2016). "I've been interviewing Norm for 18 years and he has consistently broken every talk-show rule," O'Brien says. "He tells anecdotes that are blatantly false. His stories have always been repurposed farmer's daughter routines that he swears happened to him… When Norm steps out from behind the curtain I honestly don't know what is going to happen and that electrical charge comes through the television" (Itzkoff, 2011). O'Brien has elsewhere characterized Macdonald's style as 'theater of the absurd'.[34]

With news of Macdonald's death, O'Brien tweeted "Norm had the most unique comedic voice I have ever encountered and he was so relentlessly and uncompromisingly funny. I will never laugh that hard again."[35]

His style of comedy began to change during the 2000s, towards a more pointed, almost Kaufman-esque irreverence and willingness to frustrate the audience. As a late night guest, Macdonald would venture into 'shaggy dog stories' that can easily turn into joke-suicide

---

[34] *Conan O'Brien Needs a Friend*, Interview with David Letterman, October 7, 2019, https://podcasts.apple.com/us/podcast/40-david-letterman/id1438054347?i=1000452586161

[35] https://twitter.com/ConanOBrien/status/1437863451980808192

territory, with his long and elaborate setups leading towards cheesy punchlines, jokes that are less about content than the delivery itself.[36] His Canadian 'average white guy' affability and sensibility (which may be why Indiana-born David Letterman was his staunchest defender) often made it sound like he was winging it, that he was just figuring out the joke as he told it, but this aspect of his delivery was partially deliberate. "I generally have a real strong idea or a strong punchline," he said in an interview, "and I just try to get to it by rambling around, as I don't like to memorize words. And I can't be naturalistic enough to make it sound real. So instead, I just wander around aimlessly knowing that I'll be funny enough with stream of consciousness until I get to the actual explosively funny part" (Heisler, 2011).

Chairman of the B-O-R-E-D

Macdonald's most viral guest appearance was probably in 1997 on *Late Night with Conan O'Brien*.[37] After his own segment being interviewed by Conan, Macdonald moves over to the left chair while fellow guest Courtney Thorne-Smith comes out for her interview. As he was wont to do whenever there was more than one guest on a show, Macdonald proceeds to hijack the segment.

Thorne-Smith was there to promote her upcoming movie with prop comic Carrot Top, who other stand-up comics widely consider one of the worst stand-ups to attain great success. Conan – feigning jealousy that she's made a movie with Carrot Top instead of himself, a fellow red-head – asks her if there was any kissing involved. Thorne-Smith plays along and says "Yeah, lots of making out. Nothing but making out. It's like *9½ Weeks*, but Carrot Top." The audience laughs, and then Macdonald asks: "Is it called *9½ Seconds*?" The audience laughs some more and, in the vintage Macdonald style, he unnecessarily 'explains' the joke, which works as a punchline to the punchline: "Like he's a premature ejaculator".

When Conan asks Thorne-Smith what the Carrot Top movie is going to be called, Macdonald jumps in. "I know what it's going to be

---

[36] Macdonald's "Kojak" joke that he tells to Jerry Seinfeld (*Comedians in Cars Getting Coffee*, Jan 12, 2017) is a good example of this; there is no punchline per se, it's all about the journey of his delivery.

[37] *Late Night with Conan O'Brien*, May 15, 1997, https://youtu.be/bKmadR4Ye54.

called. If it's got Carrot Top in it, you know what a good name for it would be?" he asks rhetorically, and then doing the Macdonald lean-in, answers: "Box Office Poison!".

Thorne-Smith tells Conan that the movie is titled *Chairman of the Board*, and Conan then looks at Macdonald and says "Do something with *that*, you freak." The audience laughs (at Macdonald's expense, but he is laughing too) and then after a few beats turns to Conan and says: "I bet the Board is spelled B-O-R-E-D."

The Moth Joke

One of Macdonald's more famous long jokes, and the single joke that is most identified with him, is the "Moth Joke" which he told on Conan O'Brien's show in 2009.[38] In *Based on a True Story*, Macdonald provides an extended version of the joke, replete with Russian literary angst:

> A moth goes into a podiatrist's office. The podiatrist says, "What's the problem?"
> The moth says, "Where do I begin with my problems? Every day I go to work for Gregory Vassilievich, and all day

---

[38] *The Tonight Show with Conan O'Brien*, August 31, 2009, https://www.youtube.com/watch?v=YxD3pT8C9-A.

long I toil. But what is my work? I am a bureaucrat, and so every day I joylessly move papers from one place to another and then back again. I no longer know what it is that I actually do, and I don't even know if Gregory Vassilievich knows. He only knows that he has power over me, and this seems to bring him much happiness. And where is my happiness? It is when I awake in the morning and I do not know who I am. In that single moment I am happy. In that single moment, before the memory of who I am strikes me like a cane. And I take to the streets and walk, in a malaise, here and then there and then here again. And then it is time for work. Others stopped asking me what I do for a living long ago, for they know I will have no answer and will fix my empty eyes upon them, and they fear my melancholia might prove so deep as to be contagious. Sometimes, Doc, in the deepest dark of night, I awake in my bed and I turn to my right, and with horror I see some old lady lying on my arm. An old lady that I once loved, Doc, in whose flesh I once found splendor and now see only decay, an old lady who insults me by her very existence.

"Once, Doc, when I was young, I flew into a spider web and was trapped. In my panic, I smashed my wings till the dust flew from them, but it did not free me and only alerted the spider. The spider moved toward me and I became still, and the spider stopped. I had heard many stories from my elders about spiders, about how they would sink their fangs into your cephalothorax and you would be paralyzed but aware as the spider slowly devoured you. So I remained as still as possible, but when the spider again began moving toward me, I smashed my wing again into my cage of silk, and this time it worked. I cut into the web and freed myself and flew skyward. I was free and filled with joy, but this joy soon turned to horror: I looked down and saw that in my escape I had taken with me a single strand of silk, and at the end of the strand was the spider, who was scrambling upward toward me. Was I to die high in the sky, where no spider should be? I flew this way, then that, and finally I freed myself from the strand and watched as it floated earthward with the spider. But days later a strange feeling descended upon my soul, Doc. I began to feel that my life was that single strand of silk, with a deadly spider racing up it and toward me. And I felt that I had already been bitten by his venomous fangs and that I was living in a state of paralysis, as life devoured me whole.

"My daughter, Alexandria, fell to the cold of last winter. The cold took her, as it did many of us. And so my family mourned. And I placed on my countenance the look of grief, Doc, but it was a masquerade. I felt no grief for my dead daughter but only envy. And so I have one child now, a boy, whose name is Stephan Mikhailovitch Smokovnikov, and I tell you now, Doc, with great and deep shame, the terrible truth. I no longer love him. When I look into his eyes, all I see is the same cowardice that I see when I catch a glimpse of my own eyes in a mirror. It is this cowardice that keeps me living, Doc, that keeps me moving from place to place, saying hello and goodbye, eating though hunger has long left me, walking without destination, and, at night, lying beside the strange old lady in this burlesque of a life I endure. If only the cowardice would abate for the time needed to reach over and pick up the cocked and loaded pistol that lies on my bedside table, then I might finally end this façade once and for all. But, alas, the cowardice takes no breaks; it is what defines me, it is what frames my life, it is what I am. And yet I cannot resign myself to my own life. Instead, despair is my constant companion as I walk here and then there, without dreams, without hope, and without love."

"Moth," says the podiatrist, "your tale has moved me and it is clear you need help, but it is help I cannot provide. You must see a psychiatrist and tell him of your troubles. Why on earth did you come to my office?" The moth says, "Because the light was on."

In one radio interview, Macdonald gives the backstory of the Moth Joke, calling it "an experiment born of necessity" (Power, 2016). Conan wanted to stretch Macdonald's segment past the commercial break because he loved having him as a guest, but having nothing prepared for a second segment Macdonald improvised by stretching out a short, two-line joke he'd remembered from Colin Quinn into the classic TV moment it has become.[39] By going against late-night-guest storytelling conventions and taking the time to fully anthropomorphize the moth into an angst-ridden individual -- depicting the moth as a despondent character from a bleak Russian novel by way of Kafka -- the incongruity of the punchline becomes a comedic variation of the scorpion and the frog story. "I thought if, in between this little boy's joke," Macdonald recalls, "a set of horrifying facts [was] laid end to end, then it could make the sweetness way, way funnier at the end, because they will have completely forgotten where I was" (Power, 2016). Of the joke's punchline, Dan Brooks writes:

> "It resolves the tension Macdonald has built up by situating the moth within the dynamics of human psychology and misery, slamming us back into joke territory with a reminder that, actually, it's just a moth. That's what makes us laugh, but what makes us cheer is the audacity of telling this joke on network television for three minutes, when you might be

---

[39] Macdonald also provides backstory to the Moth Joke in Edgars' 2016 "Norm Macdonald Book Tour" interview. See also Conan O'Brien's backstory account of the Moth Joke (O'Brien, 2021).

expected to use that time to promote your own career" (Brooks, 2018).

Jacques De Gatineau

Another terrific example of Macdonald's long form "storytelling" jokes is his "Jacques De Gatineau" joke (aka the "Porpoise" joke) which he told on Conan's show in 2014.[40] In this case, the long setup involves a fictional fellow Canadian named "Jacques De Gatineau". Macdonald starts the joke by referring to the man as "Jacque De Gautier," but mid-joke changes the name to "Jacques De Gatineau". When Conan calls him out on the name discrepancy (to the audience's laughter), Macdonald doesn't miss a beat: "Well, you know, a man grows." In any event, "Jacques De Gatineau" was a man whose intellectual promise was the hope of those who grew up with him in the small Canadian town they were all from. De Gatineau goes on to receive multiple degrees at McGill University… and then vanishes. Years later, Norm is visiting a SeaWorld at Niagara Falls, and in the area where they feed the baby dolphins, he sees De Gatineau feeding the baby dolphins:

> "And I go up to him and I say 'Jacques De Gatineau, I feel shame for you! You were our hope!... You were to be a great man, Jacques De Gatineau!... All of Temiscaming, Quebec pinned our hopes on you!'…
>
> Now, that's a helluva burden for a man, to have a town's hope pinned on them, isn't it Conan?
>
> So, he was feeding these baby dolphins, you know? And I said 'I'm ashamed of you Jacques De Gatineau!. You could have done so many great things."
>
> And he said "Well, I think I'm serving a youthful porpoise."

---

[40] *Conan*, May 21, 2014, https://youtu.be/n3LMSflEN54.

The audience's laughter is as much from the head-shaking reactions of disbelief from Conan and Andy Richter as it is from the joke's punchline.

Final Letterman Appearance

While Macdonald appeared on Conan's shows more than on David Letterman's, it was Letterman whom Macdonald most admired in the late-night comedy world. He believed that Letterman, in his prime, not only reinvented late-night comedy but impacted culture on a massive scale. It was Letterman who was Macdonald's earliest champion, and who became a mentor to Macdonald, giving him feedback and advice over the years. (In a 2016 appearance on Howard Stern's radio show, Macdonald said of David Letterman: "I really felt like he was my father figure.")[41]

It was to see David Letterman perform stand-up that a young 13-year old Norm Macdonald went to a Toronto talk show as an audience member, a story which Macdonald emotionally recounts in his own set in 2015 as *The Late Show with David Letterman*'s final stand-up performer.[42] In this appearance, now legendary, Macdonald has a tough time finishing the section about this early encounter with

---

[41] *The Howard Stern Show*, September 19, 2016, https://youtu.be/VmOTs36HFPw.

[42] *Late Show with David Letterman*, https://youtu.be/mFjEvl43zYY.

Letterman, and the tearful and emotional finale to his routine is quite moving.[43] He finishes his appearance by saying: "So, I'd just like to say: I know that Mr. Letterman is not for the mawkish and he has no truck for the sentimental. *But* if something is true," he says, turning to Letterman who is out of frame, "it is not sentimental." His voice now cracking with emotion, he concludes with: "And I say in truth… that I love you."

The audience cheers while Macdonald breaks down into tears. The band kicks into Dylan's "You're Gonna Make Me Lonesome When You Go," a song likely chosen by Macdonald as it also played when he came onstage to do his set.[44] Letterman walks over to Macdonald to thank him, and then waves good night to the audience.

---

[43] Macdonald would rarely demonstrate such feelings publicly, but another moment where he expressed discernable emotion is at a 2016 book event for *Based on a True Story*, where he is interviewed by the *Washington Post*'s Geoff Edgers. Macdonald gets quite emotional after he finishes reading aloud his story about the 'tiny white coffin,' something he says he once tragically witnessed. (Earlier chapters of *Based on a True Story*, which have to do with the young boy who ends up in the coffin, provide the necessary context for the significance of the clouds mentioned in the last sentence).

[44] The Dylan song is a bookend to Macdonald's first appearance on Letterman's show 25 years earlier, when the band played Dylan's "Like a Rolling Stone" as Macdonald appeared from behind the curtain to his stand-up. (*Late Night with David Letterman*, May 9, 1990, https://www.youtube.com/watch?app=desktop&v=8gTR1J5Koi8).

FOUR

Philosopher-Fool

Macdonald's simpleton demeanor was part of a carefully crafted persona. And although he hated the idea of comedians being viewed as 'philosophers', he *was* something of a Philosopher-Comedian or Philosopher-Fool. His attempts to grapple with the absurdity of existence and the specter of death informed much of his material, and there were hints of a wider interest in philosophy. Across Macdonald's career, one can find sprinkled references to philosophy.

Anti-Intellectualism

"The smartest comedians portray themselves as the dumbest," writes Jon Gabriel. "Norm Macdonald was the best at this sleight of hand. He graduated high school at 14, read Russian literature in his downtime, and had long philosophical discussions with clergy... Macdonald was a student of human nature first, comedy second" (Gabriel, 2021). In his profile of Macdonald, Dan Brooks writes:

> Although he is unmistakably intelligent in real life — Letterman told me he was "maybe the smartest guy in comedy" — he likes to establish a position of ignorance and then lecture his audience from it. Jerry Seinfeld described this approach to me as "sophisticated dumbness" — a technique that makes any glimpse of the real Macdonald feel thrilling. In those rare moments when he chuckles at his own joke or otherwise breaks character, we feel a rush of empathy, as though we have caught the playwright watching from the wings…

> "Norm just kind of twinkles, even when he's not playing the dumb guy," Letterman told me. "He's deadly funny, he's incredibly smart, he's wildly personable and he's peculiar" (Brooks, 2018).

As noted earlier, Macdonald was no doubt cognizant of, and carefully crafted, this aspect of his persona. "The last character you want to be," he said, "is a guy who's smarter than the audience" (Marchese, 2018).[45] He disdained elitism in all its forms, including in the world of comedians. When asked why sitcoms about working-class people are so rare, he replied: "A lot of writers come from Harvard and such, and are rich, and they write under the misapprehension that poor people are stupid. So when they do write them, they are hillbillies or rednecks or Christian idiots" (Saeur, 2011). Throughout his career, Macdonald would play the trickster by downplaying his intelligence, always projecting an outward image of himself as much less sophisticated than he actually was.

Very much the autodidact, in 2016 while promoting *Based on a True Story* he estimated he'd read at least a thousand books and says he began serious writing in his late teens (Marchese, 2016). For a time, he hosted a book club on Twitter (since deleted) that discussed classic works.[46]

---

[45] See also Macdonald's interview on *Larry King Now* (August 3, 2015), where he discusses this topic, adding that David Letterman was smart to realize this himself. https://youtu.be/gKkWVK2N4VU?t=768.

[46] A Reddit page about Macdonald's literary influences (https://www.reddit.com/r/NormMacdonald/comments/ps6jbj/norms_literary_r eferences/) points to Norm's Book Club,

(http://normsbookclub.com/), a page that appears to have compiled the books discussed.

In one interview, Macdonald points to the universality of great literature and how, due to the unchanging nature of the human condition, such literature that may be centuries old still resonates today. In the process, he also signals his introversion traits in his preference of the inner world of the mind over the outer world of experience:

> "These people know everything about the human condition. So, all you have to do is read them. It's better than experiencing things in life. That's for sure. Reading is far superior to experience because when you read, you can read a master's insights into the world that would take you forever" (MacPherson, 2012).

When Larry King asked him "What would you like to be remembered for?" one can detect a hint of emotion as Macdonald replied: "I think I wrote this book to be remembered by this book [*Based on a True Story*]. I think I'll probably write three more books in my life, and probably be most remembered as an author in my second life."[47] Elsewhere, he told an interviewer "I find myself in a predicament. All I want to do is write short stories or a book, but other things, often that I'm no good at all at, are offered me for much more money" (Horton, 2021). Had he lived longer, and exhibited less apathy and more ambition, Macdonald might have been capable of some very good literary work. His late-career stand-up style often involved a form of storytelling, but his long-form writing potential was largely untapped. In 2018, he told a reporter (in apparent seriousness, although it may have been a trickster ruse, given how he'd previously expressed hating the process of writing *Based on a True Story*) that his next writing project would be "a 600-page straight novel that he plans to publish under a pen name" (Brooks, 2018).

Philosophy Jokes

In discussing how the process of aging is gradual and imperceptible on a day-to-day basis, he once joked half-seriously that

---

[47] *Larry King Now*, October 17, 2016, https://youtu.be/7kbBlWnVjpA?t=1446.

"I used to think that if I videotaped myself every day, then I wouldn't age" (MacPherson, 2012), a notion that invokes one of Zeno's Paradoxes, the metaphysical *reductio ad absurdums* attributed to Zeno of Elea. After articulating his existential fatalism in (of all places) a morning radio show, Macdonald rationalized his fatalism with a mathematical point of reference: "A fraction of infinity is zero, no matter what the fraction is. You could live a hundred years, a thousand years, a billion years... it's all zero if it's on a continuum of eternity. So, it doesn't matter what you do or don't do."[48]

In *Hitler's Dog, Gossip and Trickery* (2017), he inverts Nietzsche's most famous aphorism "That which does not kill you makes you stronger," by saying: "That which does not kill you makes you weaker, and will probably kill you the next time it shows up." In this same special, he indirectly touches upon Camus' concept of the absurd and riffs on the role of metaphor in language, likely stemming from, or having been influenced by Lakoff & Johnson's theory of embodied knowledge (with metaphor at its core).[49]

Professor of Logic Joke

In 1996, on *Late Night with Conan O'Brien*, he told his "Professor of Logic" joke, one of his more famous long-form jokes.[50] The punchline involves an intentional logical fallacy, and reveals that Macdonald was perhaps more of a philosophy buff than he let on. The premise of the joke is 'Norm' meeting his new neighbor who happens to be a professor of logic at the 'University of Science'. Norm asks the professor what 'logic' is and the professor replies "Well, it's a kind of a pattern of syllogistic... well, it's hard to explain... why don't I give you an example." Using a line of Socratic questioning and inductive reasoning, the following exchange takes place:

> **PROFESSOR**: Let me ask you a question. Do you own a doghouse?

---

[48] *The Sarah & Vinnie Show*, Interview with Norm Macdonald, August 31, 2009, https://youtu.be/zSQj2HIpA7Y?t=2825.

[49] In since-deleted tweets, Macdonald commented on Lakoff. See Russell (2017) for discussion of the philosophical content of this stand-up special.

[50] https://youtu.be/Oseqh7SMIvo

NORM: Yes, I do.

PROFESSOR: Well, that means you probably have a dog.

NORM: Yes.

PROFESSOR: Well, that means you likely have a family.

NORM: Yes, I do.

PROFESSOR: Well, that means you've got kids. You're married?

NORM: Yes, I am.

PROFESSOR: Well, then you're a heterosexual man.

NORM: Yes, I am.

PROFESSOR: Well, you see, that's logic. Simply from finding out you had a doghouse, I made this series of inferences and I found that you're a heterosexual man… simply from the fact that you had a doghouse.

NORM: Good God, isn't that something!

Norm and the professor then part ways. Later, Norm is at the bus stop waiting for the bus along with some other people. Macdonald continues the joke:

I walk down to the bus stop and I'm still thinking about this thing that happened to me. There's no bus coming at all. Five or six of us are standing around. One guy lights up a cigarette and he goes 'As soon as you light up a cigarette, the bus comes.' He smokes the whole damn cigarette and no bus comes. I said to the guy 'Well, that theory really worked', and the guy goes 'Well… *sometimes* it works.'

Anyway, the guy goes 'What's new with you?' And I said 'Well, I had an interesting thing happen to me today – I met my neighbor… He has an interesting job, he's a professor of logic down at the University of Science. The guy says 'Is that so? Professor of logic? What the hell is that? Logic?'

I said 'Well, it's a series of syllo-something-or-other… I can't remember exactly, but I'll give you an example.' So the guy goes 'Alright, fair enough.'

So, I said 'Let me ask you a question. Do you own a doghouse?' And the guy goes 'No, I don't own a doghouse.'

So, I says to the guy, I says, 'Oh yeah? You're one of them gays.'

Note the digression in this joke – the part about 'if you light a cigarette, the bus will come' – which serves no real purpose other than to reveal Macdonald's knowledge of causal fallacies (e.g., transductive reasoning).

Deeply Closeted Liar's Paradox

His "deeply closeted gay man" joke is a play on the Liar's Paradox. The paradox, which goes back to Ancient Greek philosophy, involves propositions that, if they are true, are false, and vice-versa. Take the proposition "This sentence is false". If true, then it means the sentence is simultaneously false which is paradoxical. Similarly, take the proposition "I am lying." If true, then it too means that the sentence is simultaneously false, a contradiction. (Through his interest in mathematics, Macdonald may have also been familiar with Gödel's incompleteness theorem, which has a kinship to the Liar's Paradox).

In a 2016 appearance on Conan O'Brien's show[51] to promote his book *Based on a True Story*, Conan asks Macdonald if there is anything salacious about him that people might not know about:

---

[51] *Conan*, October 6, 2016, https://youtu.be/L7K-kaelQEs?t=60.

NORM: I guess the biggest thing that nobody knows about me is that I'm a deeply closeted gay man.

CONAN: What? You're a gay man?

NORM: I'm not gay! I said I'm deeply closeted! I'm as straight as an arrow!

CONAN: So, you're a gay man who won't admit it.

NORM: No, no. Do you know what 'deeply closeted' means? It means a man who will not acknowledge that he's gay. So, I'm telling you -- I'm not gay!

What is it Like to be a Chicken?

Although it may be a stretch, his "What is it like to be a chicken?" bit during an appearance on David Letterman's show suggests Thomas Nagel's seminal paper "What Is It Like to Be a Bat?"[52] Nagel's thesis, which forms a crucial roadblock to a reductionist theory of mind, argues that the so-called 'hard problem' in philosophy of mind (the center of the mind-body problem) may never be solved by science due to the possible irreducibility of *qualia* (i.e., the subjective experience associated with the phenomenology of conscious perception), which by analogy is why a human will never know what it is like to be a bat. As Nagel puts it:

> "[An] organism has conscious mental states if and only if there is something it is like to be that organism -- something it is like for organism... If physicalism is to be defended, the phenomenological features must themselves be given a physical account. But when we examine their subjective character it seems that such a result is impossible. The reason is that every subjective phenomenon is essentially connected with a single point of view, and it seems inevitable that an objective, physical theory will abandon that point of view...any shift to greater objectivity -- that is, less attachment

---

[52] https://youtu.be/VtLL3LOi87I

to a specific viewpoint -- does not take us nearer to the real nature of the phenomenon: it takes us farther away from it" (Nagel, 1974).

In his chicken bit, Macdonald recounts how as a child he saw a magician named Reveen the Impossiblist who would hypnotize audience members, convincing one that he was a chicken:

> **NORM**: I was sitting there in the aisle with my brother and the guy that thought he was a chicken came running by me, pecking at things, 'cluck-cluck-cluck' and all this… After the show, I go out in the parking lot and I see the guy that was the chicken. So I walk up to the guy and I go 'Man, how did that feel? It must have been amazing to feel like a chicken,' and he goes 'Oh, it was cool.'
>
> **DAVE**: Really.
>
> **NORM** [*with an expression of suspicion*]: So, then I thought 'I don't know'… You know? Because imagine if for 15 minutes you thought you were a chicken, right? Then afterwards you'd be like [*holds the following expression for several beats*]:

[*Resumes talking*]: He'd have to spend the rest of his life trying to get back on track, because his mind had been shattered!

DAVE: Shattered by the experience of being a chicken?

NORM: Well, of course! If you thought for 10 minutes that you were *actually* a chicken, would you be able to do the show the next night?!

Intuitionism

One should not expect from Macdonald a tight and coherent epistemology that has been carefully mapped out. He found it ridiculous that anyone would look to a comedian (or an actor) for philosophical enlightenment (MacPherson, 2012). That being said, he seemed attuned to issues of warranted belief and loosely articulated an anti-realist position. He was certainly opposed to both scientific reductionism and scientism (the belief that empirical science is the only arbiter of knowledge).[53] Anti-realism applies to claims about the ontological status of unobservable entities such as electrons or DNA, which are not detectable with human senses but require intermediary, constructed instruments. Influenced by Wittgenstein, Michael Dummett was the analytic philosopher who coined the phrase 'anti-realism' in this philosophy of science context, and who posited a key epistemological role for intuitionism.

Macdonald himself placed great value on intuition and seemed to imply that intuitive aspects of subjective experience can be valid forms of truth, or at least that imagination is as integral to truth as sense datum experience. Likewise, he extended the concept of 'faith' to be applicable not just to religious beliefs but also to certain scientific beliefs, namely our everyday beliefs about unobservable entities, which often involve a level of trust or faith of sorts. When asked about his religious faith, Macdonald replied: "There's a lot of things I have faith [in]… but I don't really 'believe' in DNA… I don't have faith in science… Haven't scientists always been wrong? They

---

[53] The most sustained discussion on these philosophical topics by Macdonald are in MacPherson (2021). They are also briefly discussed in, of all places, his interview on *Larry King Now* (October 17, 2016), https://www.youtube.com/watch?v=7kbBIWnVjpA&t=335s.

used to think the sun went around the earth. Everybody said 'Hey, that's science'".[54]

"The scientific method always begins with intuition," Macdonald says during a discussion about the God Hypothesis (MacPherson, 2012). This sentiment echoes Karl Popper's philosophy of science as a series of conjectures and refutations – the conjectures being the creative hypotheses (which contain an element of irrationality) emerging from one's imagination, the refutations being the process of testing and falsification of the hypothesis. The criteria of falsifiability asserts that a hypothesis *must* in principle be falsifiable -- there must be an empirical process and set of conditions by which the hypothesis could in principle be proven false -- or else the hypothesis, while seeming to 'explain everything', in fact explains nothing, much like a vacuous fortune cookie message or an unfalsifiable statement such as "God causes everything" does, or that crude variants of Marxism or Freudianism similarly do (Popper, 1963).

Macdonald, however, goes on to reject falsificationism as a necessary condition of knowledge, and points to evolutionary theory itself (which Macdonald himself says he believes in) as failing to meet the strict threshold of "scientific law". About evolutionary theory, Popper himself held a similar view, believing that Darwinism (in particular, the theory of natural selection) is tautologous and ultimately an untestable scientific theory better characterized as a metaphysical research programme, although Popper would later modify his position about Darwinism's philosophical status (Popper, 1978).[55]

Of the associated *demarcation problem* in philosophy of science -- i.e., how we are able to definitely distinguish (if at all possible) 'science' from non-science -- Macdonald articulates a version of the problem from the context of atheists proclaiming 'There is no God' with absolute certainty. "I don't know when scientists began saying things are 'unknowable'", he says, "because that's not a scientific term as far as *I* know… It infers that they can see into the future." (MacPherson, 2012). Similarly, Macdonald broaches the philosophical problems with determinism (e.g., the reductive physicalism implicit in

---

[54] *Larry King Now*, May 22, 2013.
[55] For one of the more influential compendiums discussing problems with the falsifiability criterion, see Lakatos & Musgrave (1970).

applied science) and associated problems with naturalized epistemology (such as evolutionary epistemology):

> "If everything was created by accident, then that means... Richard Dawkins was created by accident, so why the f*ck should I listen to him? Why would an accident be able to convey to me how he became an accident through a series of accidents? That makes no sense to me" (MacPherson, 2012).

Vis-à-vis a philosophical/theological position of intelligent design, Macdonald then sketches a philosophy of mind that displays both a computational theory of mind and a Platonic or Leibnizian concept of the soul. "I believe that man *has* a body," he says, "but man *is* a soul... The bodies that we have are no more than garments" (MacPherson, 2012).

Macdonald also extended his informal philosophical intuitionism into the domain of moral epistemology, roughly articulating a position of *ethical intuitionism* which is itself a form of moral cognitivism. As such, he rejected the moral relativism which he deemed necessarily consequential from atheism:

> "Intuition is everything to me, more than my mind, because my mind can play tricks on me. And my mind is very easily swayed by others and so forth. I personally believe that there is something else other than the mind. You can't talk me into murdering somebody with your atheistic idea [of] 'What does it matter one way or the other?'" (MacPherson, 2012).

He saw truth as distinct from facts, and asserted that his book *Based on a True Story*, insofar as it is autobiographical, contains "more truth than facts". In the Introduction to the book, he writes "I'll call it *Based on a True Story*, because it comes to me that there's no way of telling a true story. I mean a really true one, because of memory. It's just no good."

Because he found memory to be unreliable, he decided to use his imagination to tell stories that get to the 'truth' of his past and to the 'truth' of the human condition. "I thought of a way of not lying and I'll share it with you if you like," he says in *Hitler's Dog, Gossip and Trickery* (2017), "You can tell the truth -- word for word, absolutely true -- but when you do it... you use a sarcastic accent." *Based on a*

True Story contains a chapter titled "The Final Chapter" (which isn't actually the final chapter) which begins: "There is the way things are and then the way things appear, and it is the way things appear, even when false, that is often the truest." In a wonderful passage about personal identity that follows, Macdonald presents himself as an example, weaving the chapter's opening sentence around his own 'You're the guy from SNL' identity. "It can be difficult to define yourself by something that happened so long ago and is gone forever," he writes. "It's like a fellow at the end of the bar telling no one in particular about the silver medal he won in high school track, the one he still wears around his neck."[56]

Given Macdonald's suspicions of empiricism, and his early proclivities for math, it should come as no surprise that he liked the purity of mathematics. "In math, you could get 100 percent," he is attributed with saying. "It was very fair. That's what I liked about math. You could figure it out, and the teacher couldn't have a stupid opinion about it."[57] In 2016, he admitted than an OCD behavior of his since childhood, which he still had, involved flipping coins and recording the outcome, which suggests an interest in probability and may be tied to his lifelong gambling addiction.[58]

Norm Macdonald ✓
@normmacdonald

Hey, guys I understand completely. When I finally understood the underpinnings of crypto, it was one of the most edifying moments. It is so deep, please dive in. I studied six months eight hours a day and what a joy. And I hope you get as lucky as I did as a result. Peace.

5:43 AM · Jan 17, 2021 · Twitter Web App

---

[56] At a 2016 book event for *Based on a True Story*, Macdonald reads this short chapter aloud. The emotion we see on his face upon finishing is quite moving. (Edgers, "Norm Macdonald Book Tour" interview, 2016, https://www.youtube.com/watch?v=oU81p6RN6b8&t=2478s).

[57] https://www.brainyquote.com/quotes/norm_macdonald_557257.

[58] See his interview on *Larry King Now* (October 17, 2016), https://youtu.be/7kbBIWnVjpA?t=335. Macdonald has also said "I'm getting some late-onset OCD, I think, because I count everything now" (Matthews, 2016).

FIVE

Litterateur

Literary Influences

Collating some of Macdonald's prodigious Twitter output (which he would typically delete in short order), Lili Loofbourow provides us with valuable insight into some of his literary and other interests and influences:

> He loved golf and David Letterman and Alice Munro and hated Bret Easton Ellis and really hated Margaret Atwood. He took a dim view of political humor (except when it was about the Clintons being murderers), admired Bob Dylan and Steven Pinker and Jordan Peterson and Cormac McCarthy, found Noam Chomsky too difficult and George Lakoff too easy, and disliked jokes about Christianity and the Bible (Loofbourow, 2021).

Regarding Jordan Peterson, Macdonald was a big fan of the fellow Canadian before Peterson became an international phenomenon:

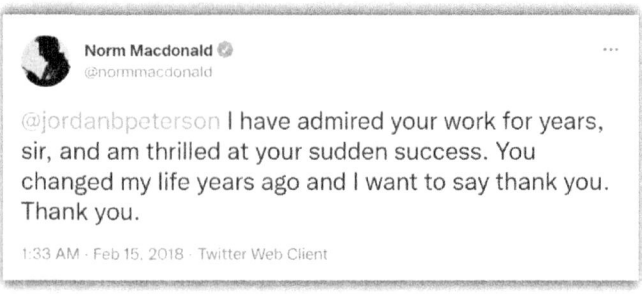

Macdonald was an avid fan of outlaw country singer-songwriter Billy Joe Shaver, considering him "the best writer in America" (MacPherson, 2012). The two would become friends, and Macdonald had Shaver as a guest on his Netflix show *Norm Macdonald Has a Show*. Macdonald especially loved Shaver's song "I'm Just an Old Chunk of Coal (But I'm Gonna Be a Diamond Someday)", and throughout his career would frequently refer to himself as "this old chunk of coal."[59]

Macdonald repeatedly cited Tolstoy as his favorite author, and he often praised Chekhov, but didn't care much for Dostoevsky:

Norm Macdonald ✅
@normmacdonald

Dostoevsky was far the inferior to Tolstoy, he was inferior to most of the great Russians.

12:43 AM · Feb 9, 2016 · Twitter Web Client

Norm Macdonald ✅
@normmacdonald

Dosto is a fine writer. Better are Tolstoy, Chekhov, Gogol, Turgenev and Pushkin.

1:30 AM · Feb 9, 2016 · Twitter Web Client

Norm Macdonald ✅
@normmacdonald   ···

Chekhov's short stories. All great If it's just one pick, I guess Ward#6.

Kristina @Creature_Kris · Nov 24, 2016
@normmacdonald read Tolstoy because of your recommendation. If you have others, I'd love to look into them.

1:48 AM · Nov 24, 2016 · Twitter Web Client

---

[59] Macdonald was a big fan of outlaw country music. See his 2011 interview of fellow country music fan Robert Duvall, when Macdonald was guest-hosting for *The Dennis Miller Show*, https://youtu.be/3ltgCsd3BMg.

That his favorite Chekhov story would be "Ward No. 6" is in line with his bleak fatalism. The story's protagonist is a doctor beleaguered with an unalterable existential crisis. Knowledge of the inevitability of death, and how one's existence will soon be completely forgotten with the passage of time overwhelms the protagonist, making the everyday banality of small-talk unbearable to him. He yearns for intellectual conversation, and is only able to find it with a patient at the insane asylum where the doctor works. The sentiments expressed by the doctor are very much in line with sentiments Macdonald expressed in his material and in interviews.

Macdonald liked Dylan Thomas, Jack London, J.D. Salinger, William Faulkner, and Philip Roth. He liked Proust and Raymond Carver (Parker, 2016). He felt that Charles Portis was the greatest comic novelist since Mark Twain (Domenech, 2021).

He liked Thomas Pynchon, and in 2017 tweeted the following tease, with his characteristic elusiveness capping off the short thread:

That Macdonald would be excited about this invitation makes perfect sense: Pynchon and McCarthy (who are both also reclusive and notoriously averse to publicity) are first class wordsmiths whose work often involves either made-up portmanteaus (Pynchon) or obscure and esoteric word selection (McCarthy). Given that Pynchon lives in L.A., where Macdonald lived, and given their mutual connection to creators of *The Simpsons*, it seems likely that Macdonald was referring to Pynchon, although a tweet he posted the following year suggests it may have been McCarthy:

Norm Macdonald ✓
@normmacdonald

my good friend Cormac is the only one. And, of course, Alice Munro, whom I've never met.

Alex Fokken @alexanderognes · Nov 6, 2018
Hey @normmacdonald, do you have any favorite modern/current day authors?

7:01 AM · Nov 6, 2018 · Twitter Web Client

Macdonald's implicit literary criticism applied an ethical dimension to the aesthetic, and he could be quite strident in his opinions. Of Margaret Atwood's leftwing, feminist, dystopian novel (the source of endless public AWFL cosplay), he tweeted:

Norm Macdonald ✓
@normmacdonald

I've just read an incredible article where "The Handmaid's Tale", a sub-par piece of science-fi trash, is defended by its author.

5:49 PM · Apr 26, 2017 · Twitter Web Client

When Bret Easton Ellis, whose fiction tends to wallow in amorality and decadence, once dismissed Alice Munro as a writer,

Macdonald took to Twitter to launch a blistering salvo against him (Diamond, 2021)[60]:

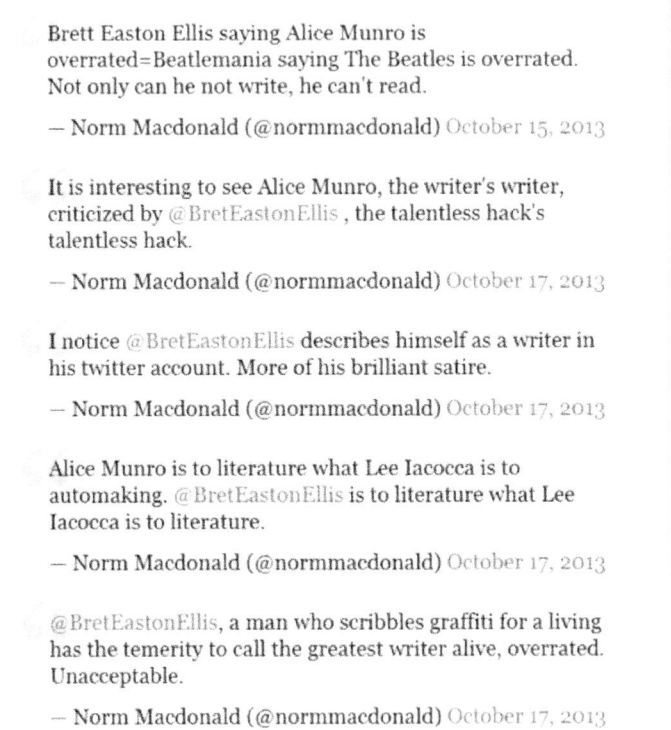

Brett Easton Ellis saying Alice Munro is overrated=Beatlemania saying The Beatles is overrated. Not only can he not write, he can't read.

— Norm Macdonald (@normmacdonald) October 15, 2013

It is interesting to see Alice Munro, the writer's writer, criticized by @BretEastonEllis, the talentless hack's talentless hack.

— Norm Macdonald (@normmacdonald) October 17, 2013

I notice @BretEastonEllis describes himself as a writer in his twitter account. More of his brilliant satire.

— Norm Macdonald (@normmacdonald) October 17, 2013

Alice Munro is to literature what Lee Iacocca is to automaking. @BretEastonEllis is to literature what Lee Iacocca is to literature.

— Norm Macdonald (@normmacdonald) October 17, 2013

@BretEastonEllis, a man who scribbles graffiti for a living has the temerity to call the greatest writer alive, overrated. Unacceptable.

— Norm Macdonald (@normmacdonald) October 17, 2013

"Alice Munro doesn't wallow in self-pity," he told an interviewer years later. "Alice Munro finds beauty in what she writes, and that's what every artist does because life sucks, you know?" (Marchese, 2018).

---

[60] Another tweet from this barrage was: "@BretEastonEllis Do you think Alice Munro is overrated because you never see her at one of John Casablanca's ecstasy parties" (Shah, 2013). Macdonald once described Ellis' writing as "graffiti" (CBC, "Norm Macdonald in Studio Q", February 2, 2015, https://youtu.be/wxuFAeOe4FI?t=209). The two appear to have made amends, however, as a few years later Ellis would interview Macdonald and had kind words to say about him (*The Bret Easton Ellis Show*, February 15, 2019, https://youtu.be/HxCGf9E3ffU).

Meeting Bob Dylan

"He was kinda like the Bob Dylan of comedy," said Jay Leno after Macdonald's death. "He was doing lyrics and words and phrases that nobody else in comedy was using. And it wasn't that he told jokes as much as just told stories in a funny way and had a funny inflection… Everybody else wrote jokes; he talked funny… He was almost like a jazz comedian, in that you really had to listen to him. And the people who were detractors just weren't listening."[61]

A huge Bob Dylan fan, Macdonald read biographies of the singer-songwriter and began to adopt more elaborate, Dylan-esque techniques of biographical elusiveness and trickster behavior. His tale of meeting the legendary songwriting wordsmith is a good example of Macdonald's literary flair and artistic ambition, especially as the two discussed the nature of writing and the possibility of words. It turns out that Bob Dylan is a fan of Macdonald's and in 2015 he invited Macdonald to his house for a marathon two-day conversation. Macdonald later tweeted (and then deleted)[62] a general account of this meeting, but the full twitter thread showcased a side to Macdonald's writing that would most fully be on display in *Based on a True Story*, that is, a style where (much like Dylan himself) truth and embellishment are woven together for a metafiction effect. Here is just part of his thread:

> When Bob Dylan speaks, his words seem chosen long ago, his sentences are spare, and he looks right at you, and his countenance is stone. He spoke to me for many hours over two days. There was no alcohol or drugs consumed. He was interested only in writing. I remember wishing I had secretly recorded him, and I remember trying as hard as I could to remember every word he said. I remember he talked over and over about verbs and about 'verbifying', how anything could be 'verbified'. He asked me my favorite book of the Bible and I said Job, and he said his favorite was Ecclesiastes. He then

---

[61] *The Tim Conway Jr Show*, September 15, 2021, https://podbay.fm/p/conway-on-demand/e/1631683649.

[62] A prolific tweeter, Macdonald would often delete tweets, sometimes just hours after posting them.

told me that the book of Job I was familiar with was not the original, and then he told me the original.

I began to notice his speech was naturally rich with imagery, and that listening to him had a mesmerizing effect. I noticed when looking at his face while listening to his words that it was like looking at an impressionistic painting. I cannot repeat any of what I heard that evening, but he invited me to stay the night and we ate dinner in silence. A girl cooked a beef stew and there were three other men, who I later learned were musicians. When Bob Dylan retired for the evening, I spoke freely with the three men. They took me to a recording studio in a guest house and I listened to them play. I asked them for their favorite Dylan stories. They told me, and the night happened and I didn't sleep. I was very unknown at the time and asked why Bob Dylan had summoned me for this visit. One of the men told me.

Lili Loofbourow similarly recounts this story (also recounted by Brooks, 2018) and juxtaposes it against Macdonald's alleged second interaction with Dylan on an L.A. sidewalk. In this second encounter (it's unclear whether it took place before or after the stayover at Dylan's home), Dylan either doesn't yet know or doesn't recognize Macdonald, and simply asks him for a light to his cigarette, as one might with any stranger. Regarding these two Dylan tales, Loofbourow writes:

In one, Dylan doesn't just recognize Norm; he plucks him out of comparative obscurity, mentors and tutors him, talks to him for hours, and changes his life. In the second, they barely interact. That's deep play. Lonely play. It's comedy not actually pitched to an audience. Who knows if either version is true -- the deep communion or the casual anti-communion with Dylan where nothing of value was said. It's the kind of game a bullshit artist plays all by himself, enjoying the fact that no one else need ever get the joke (Loofbourow, 2021).

With either of these stories (or both), was Macdonald perhaps deploying the Dylan-esque tactic of masking, of being the media trickster? Whether or not either of these Dylan stories is true,

Macdonald *would* spend the better part of his life engaging in his own masking strategies, designed both to throw people off the trail of his true biography and to bolster his crafted public persona. The definitive example of this is the one book he published, *Based on a True Story*.

Based on a True Story

The hidden depths of Macdonald's intellectual streak and literary ability are on full display in his extremely funny and well-received semi-fictional memoir *Based on a True Story* (2016).[63] Anyone reading (or, ideally, listening to) this book expecting a conventional celebrity memoir is in for a surprise; it is more a farcical novel, with the occasional current of genuine memoir laced into (although via a narrator of uncertain reliability) what is otherwise a funny, moving, and surprisingly deep work of fiction. As noted earlier, Macdonald was a rather private person, who felt uncomfortable discussing himself, especially any unseemly aspects of his past or present, and this aversion to discuss such things in the 'confessional' style is in line with his general outlook on life.[64] Instead, he obscures, hints at, and alludes to.

With us now knowing that he wrote the book while in the middle of a leukemia illness that would eventually take his life, one can see strings of clues and indirect references to his experience with cancer, and to the fear-of-death that this illness brought to the foreground of his consciousness. For instance, one of the epigraphs of the book is a Tolstoy quote from *War and Peace*: "I know of only two very real evils in life: remorse and illness."

---

[63] It is highly recommended to listen to this book as an audiobook. Macdonald himself does the reading, and the quintessential Macdonald cadence, inflections, and comedic timing are otherwise lost.

[64] Of confessional comedy, Macdonald has said: "That doesn't really even have a place in social intercourse. Confessional is meant to be something you do in a dark booth beside a holy man and whispered" (Marchese, 2016).

In a particularly grim chapter involving Macdonald agreeing to help a terminally ill child fulfill his wish, he says of the child at one point: "I gave him his pills… so many pills," something Macdonald no doubt had familiarity with.

Nonetheless, we are left to speculate as to which particular anecdotes in *Based on a True Story* are completely true, which are partially true, and which are not true at all. The more fantastic storylines in the book (e.g., serving 40 years in prison) are obviously false but make for hilarious and ripping yarns. The book fluctuates in literary style across various chapters, and is primarily in the mold of 50s/60s-era (and unfortunately-named) 'postmodernist literature'. It is mostly told in the style of Hunter S. Thompson's *Fear and Loathing in Las Vegas*, although one can detect the influences of Burroughs, Pynchon and Vonnegut as well.[65] There's also certain stylizations in the mold of Laurence Sterne's *Tristam Shandy*, a book Macdonald liked. Comic digressions, colorful characters, and vivid metaphors abound in *Based on a True Story*. There is a metafictive aspect to the book as well, when a fictional ghostwriter of the very book we are reading occasionally interjects, harkening to the Charles Kinbote character in Nabokov's *Pale Fire*, a book that Macdonald loved.

To varying degrees, and at various levels, the book's predominant themes have to do with the absurdity of existence and the fear of death, but expressed through a wild, surreal gambling trip and various other side diversions. Through the primary character of the book – that of Norm himself – one can discern a cloud of depression and melancholia, with some characters contemplating or even attempting suicide, the latter invariably failing to comic effect.[66] On a lesser plain, there are indirect critiques of our celebrity-worshipping culture,

---

[65] Macdonald's columns for *Grantland* (https://grantland.com/contributors/norm-macdonald/) contain seeds for some of the Hunter S. Thompson-like escapades of *Based on a True Story*. His long-running references to 'finding' Adam Eget under the Queensboro Bridge doing degrading things (mentioned in *Based on a True Story* and in many of Macdonald's podcasts) is a lift from Kurt Vonnegut's *Breakfast of Champions* (1973). "The next thing he knew," begins a passage in the Vonnegut novel, "he was on his hands and knees underneath the Queensboro Bridge at Fifty-ninth Street, with the East River nearby."

[66] That Macdonald might have been a depressive should come as no surprise, not only due to his lifelong struggles with cancer, but due to the fact that many of the comedy greats were depressives off-stage. See, for instance, Kevin Pollak's documentary *Misery Loves Comedy* (2013), which is about this subject.

the fickle nature of show business, and the understated role of luck in our lives.

When juxtaposed against media profiles about him over the years, certain anecdotes in *Based on a True Story* are, in all likelihood, true: how he began doing stand-up, how he was mentored by Sam Kinison, how he stumbled into getting his SNL gig… these are all accounted for. There is one brief, unexpected, and quite dark episode that is told: Macdonald the fabulist would claim he grew up on a small, failed Canadian farm, but his book contains a cryptic and fantastically-written rendition of what may have been sexual abuse he experienced by "Old Jack", a "farmhand" who lived on the "family farm".

The only other rather disturbing scene in the book – which he fought with his book editor to keep (Munroe, 2016) -- is the jarring 'seal clubbing' sequence in a section of the book dealing with a terminally-ill-child. The dying boy's wish is, unexpectedly, to club a baby seal, and the sequence is clearly taken from Jack London's *The Sea Wolf*, a book that Macdonald admired and that London wrote based on his actual experiences as a 17-year old working for a bloody and cruel seal-hunting expedition. In Macdonald's book, the bloodlust that accompanies the actualization of the boy's wish miraculously 'cures' him, but the boy is tragically killed shortly thereafter, struck by a bus while crossing a NYC street. In depicting this 'cure', Macdonald may be toying here with causal fallacies (such as the digression in his Moth Joke where a man at the bus stop says "When you light a cigarette, the bus comes"). From another angle, the irony of the boy beating his disease but being killed by a bus exemplifies the pure contingencies of life and fate. Macdonald may also be alluding here to Sam Kinison, whom Macdonald greatly admired, and who was killed after being struck by a drunk driver. As far as why he would insert a brief but concentrated description of the brutal killing of a baby seal, which is a rather incongruent scene in *Based on a True Story*, Macdonald may also be using shock tactics to voice his objection to trophy-hunting.

While not a vegetarian, there is a discernable concern for the animal kingdom in his later material and social media posts. In his 2017 stand-up special *Hitler's Dog, Gossip and Trickery*, he references a female friend who provides solid ethical arguments against eating meat (his very close friend and producing partner Lori Jo Hoekstra is a vegetarian), to which Macdonald says he's only able to reply [*assumes dumb guy voice*]: "I like pork." His "Life-Saving Pig" long-form joke seems to have an active ethical backdrop to its punchline.[67] Macdonald would later attempt to articulate, however briefly, an argument for 'ethical hunting'. In a Twitter exchange with Ricky Gervais (who is a vegetarian) on the subject of trophy-hunting, Macdonald voiced his disapproval of the practice and further tweeted: "Hunting for food is an entirely different idea. I see hunting for food as ethically better than shopping for meat."[68] This seems to be part of a pattern of the increased empathy he expressed on all fronts in his final years. (One Reddit account of how in 2017 he handled a particularly aggressive heckler is, if true, quite moving.)[69]

---

[67] *Late Night with Conan O'Brien*, March 21, 1996, https://youtu.be/vATVsdYLRT0.

[68] https://twitter.com/normmacdonald/status/1011364656672149504

[69] https://www.reddit.com/r/NormMacdonald/comments/pryq18/an_unknown_story_about_norms_humanity/

SIX

Politics

Macdonald kept his politics close to the vest, and he may have been politically aloof ("I don't know anything about politics. Like, zero. Nothing"), but one could discern a decidedly conservative streak in his general cultural outlook. "He was cagey about his politics," writes Loofbourow, "though a rightward tilt was discernible and what few firm positions he took publicly sometimes seemed more personality-driven than principled" (Loofbourow, 2021). In a 2012 interview, when asked about the inscrutability of his politics, Macdonald replied: "I have some beliefs that are too inflammatory to even discuss... unfortunately. Because there are certain things in society that you are not allowed to believe or speak [about] publicly, and so I'll just never say them. I'll just leave them in my little head" (MacPherson, 2012).

That being said, he was occasionally brazen and over time became more willing to publicly articulate certain positions. He was merciless on the Clintons, and had a particular loathing of Hillary Clinton. (See his years of references to Vince Foster).[70] His funny routine at the 1997 White House Correspondents Dinner shows he was more politically astute than he typically displayed.[71] He dared to say positive things about Republican Presidents and criticized the impeachment frenzy that surrounded Trump's Presidency (Capshaw, 2018). When asked directly about abortion, he voiced pro-life sentiments (Hochman, 2021). There are Carl Schmitt overtones when he says of sports: "I don't really like politics that much. And I like the order and simplicity of sports... It's like a war construct, except nobody has guns. You can't love your team without hating another team" (Saeur, 2011). At a 2014 low-budget YouTube red carpet event, when Sarah Silverman describes her Jash channel as a "comedy collective", Macdonald interjects and says "No offense, but it sounds

---

[70] https://youtu.be/_DyafqsZa7M
[71] https://youtu.be/3U7AZIdalzM

like some f*cking Commie goobledy-gook… I mean, I've never heard the word 'collective' without Leon Trotsky".[72]

Overall, however, as the years passed he refrained from any overt political content in his humor, believing political topicality severely dated a comedian's material. In an interview promoting his 2018 Netflix show, Macdonald expresses his general disdain of satire and preference for parody, and laments the politicization of contemporary late night talk shows:

> "It was important to me that we not do anything political. [Johnny] Carson went through Vietnam and Watergate and I don't think he ever addressed either thing. And that's all right… I don't really like satire. I think it's very minor; I think parody is very major comedy. Like, Nabokov to me is the highest form of parody… So I don't like satire that much, and also these guys [contemporary talk-show hosts] are nightclub comics. They're not Bob Dylan. They're just guys, and they get talk shows and suddenly they're telling me how I shouldn't be sad because of the Manchester bombing and I can escape the horrors of life because they're going to interview someone from *Two Broke Girls* or whatever the f*ck they do… I keep hearing how great Lenny Bruce and Bill Hicks and Mort Sahl are. People have their own taste, but to me, all three of those people are just shit. They're not comedians in my mind" (Marchese, 2018).

In crafting his material, Macdonald instead sought a purer form of comedy and hoped to create material that would be found funny long after it is initially created:

> "[W]hat I want to do is always make my stand-up and everything I do as timeless as possible, or at least not time-stamped. I'll never talk about a politician or an issue, because I want the show to work 20 years from now. Secondly, as odd as it sounds, I want my show to be comic relief from the talk shows that already exist, because now, everyone is commanded to be a political pundit as a talk-show host" (Rose, 2021).

---

[72] https://www.youtube.com/watch?v=gl6R5ROEaDY&t=600s

In his later years, it was through Macdonald's Twitter feed that one could glimpse his politics. For example, in 2017 he tweeted out a hat-tip to Tucker:

Representative of some of his rare politically-tinged humor is his Muslim backlash tweet:

Of the alarmist, Leftist, cosplay against the Trump administration that involved female protestors wearing costumes from *The Handmaid's Tale*, and their citing the dystopian novel as 'timely', Macdonald was blunt:

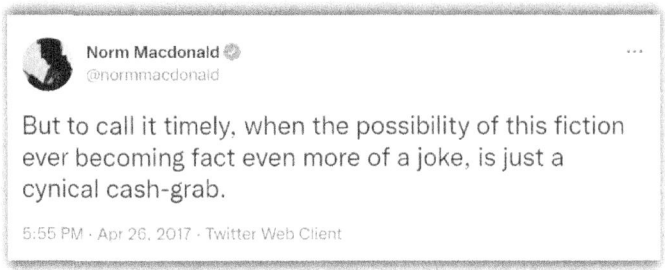

Norm Macdonald ✓
@normmacdonald   ...

But to call it timely, when the possibility of this fiction
ever becoming fact even more of a joke, is just a
cynical cash-grab.

5:55 PM · Apr 26, 2017 · Twitter Web Client

Regarding the January 6th "Insurrection" at the U.S. Capitol, Macdonald posted the following since-deleted tweet:

Norm Macdonald just Tweeted:

Norm Macdonald @normmacdonald
I loved when the violent terrorists made
sure to respect the velvet ropes in
Statuary Hall.

In 2020, he replied to someone's tweet by saying "The country is being torn apart by extremism," and then recommending the excellent Netflix documentary *The Social Dilemma* (2020):

Norm Macdonald ✓
@normmacdonald   ...

I agree, Ian. The country is being torn apart by
extremism. The Netflix doc " The Social Dilemmaq"
should be required reading. Peace, my brother.

🐻 Ian Boothby ✓ @IanBoothby · Nov 12, 2020
Replying to @normmacdonald
Right wing folks aren't automatically jerks, no. Something like Ms. Jackson's old
song seems harmless but that spreads conspiracy nonsense that has lead to a
lot of dangerous things especially with President who encourages it. Also making
a joke and a guy linked you into it.

7:47 PM · Nov 12, 2020 · Twitter Web App

Cultural Politics (Against Wokeness)

In the realm of cultural politics, however, Macdonald was relatively active. He constantly poked fun at political correctness and identity politics, and reacted against their coercive elements. As best he could in his own small way, Macdonald used his humor as a form of resistance against wokeness and creeping cultural decadence. On his Twitter account, the last tweet he 'liked' before he passed away pertained to this one:

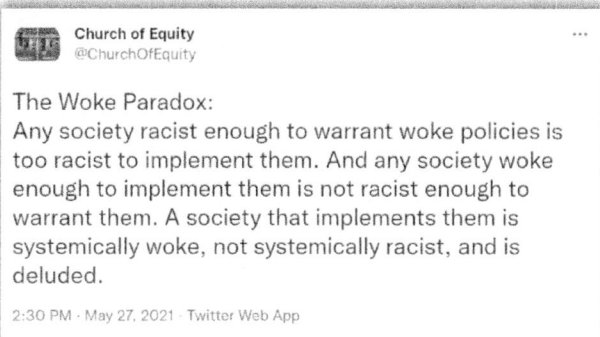

Church of Equity
@ChurchOfEquity

The Woke Paradox:
Any society racist enough to warrant woke policies is too racist to implement them. And any society woke enough to implement them is not racist enough to warrant them. A society that implements them is systemically woke, not systemically racist, and is deluded.

2:30 PM · May 27, 2021 · Twitter Web App

From even his earliest years, Macdonald's critiques of political correctness and its multitudinous manifestations could be merciless. A joke from his *Weekend Update* years: "It was revealed this week that mass murderer Richard Speck, while serving a lifetime sentence in prison, was videotaped with hormone-induced breasts, snorting cocaine and having sex with a man. The film was apparently made with prison video equipment and a $300,000 grant from the National Endowment for the Arts."

In many interviews over the years, Macdonald expressed how much he dislikes agenda-driven humor, and has characterized his repeated hammering of O.J. Simpson on *Weekend Update* as a rare instance of "moral outrage" being put into his material (Edgers, "Norm Macdonald Book Tour" interview, 2016). In *Based on a True Story*, Macdonald writes a funny, fictionalized account of his SNL firing by Don Ohlmeyer, inverting the reason for his termination. It's got all of the hallmarks of Macdonald's smirking dryness. In the book, Macdonald says Ohlmeyer fired him not for doing *too many* jokes about O.J. Simpson, but for *not doing them anymore*. In this fictional account, Ohlmeyer loves to tease O.J. on the golf course with Norm's latest O.J. joke, and now that a contrite 'Norm', wracked with guilt over his "institutionalized racism", no longer does O.J. jokes, Ohlmeyer is beside himself:

> "Norm, are you aware that I am very good friends with O. J. Simpson?"
>
> "Oh, yes, sir, I am, and I know I have been pretty hard on him on *Update*. I apologize for that. I guess where the blame really lies is in my institutionalized racism."
>
> "Oh, no, Norm, you don't understand. I never had a problem with the jokes. I loved them. I just noticed that about six months ago you stopped doing them. You never bring O.J. up at all anymore."
>
> "Well, Don, that's because a jury of his peers found Mr. Simpson not guilty of all the charges filed against him. He's as innocent as you or me. If I was to mention O.J. at all on the telecast, it would be to deliver a profound and heartfelt apology for the cruel, racist remarks I made in my self-appointed role as judge, jury, and executioner."…
>
> "If you want to save your job, Norm, get back to the O.J. jokes. You promise me that and I promise that you can have *Update* as long as you like."
>
> "I don't think I could do that, sir. What about the jury system and fair play and all that?"

'Norm' then consults with his SNL writing partners, trying to decide what to do:

> "We all agreed that what we had done to O.J. had been unconscionable. We had been mostly fueled by my lifelong institutionalized racism. Now that we'd woken up to that fact, to continue to make O.J. jokes while the real killers were at large was out of the question… The only thing O. J. Simpson was guilty of was being the best running back in history. And while O. J. Simpson had proven himself to be the greatest rusher, I had proven myself to be the greatest rusher to judgment.

Against Confessional Comedy

As noted earlier, Macdonald in later years would frequently express how much he disliked 'confessional comedy' (insofar as the form can be properly construed as 'comedy' and not something else) which had become vogue in the 2000s. Given his own cancer illness, we can partly explain in hindsight his aversion to this stand-up form due to its being antithetical to the stoicism and fatalism he indirectly articulated over the years:

"I do not like confessional comedy. I don't like it at all. Nothing can be easier than being confessional. Confessional is bragging. That's all it is… People think things are tragedy. They're not tragedy. If you get cancer, that's not a tragedy. If your mother dies when she's 30, that's not tragedy. That's life. You don't yell it from the rooftops. It has no place in comedy" (Marchese, 2016)

In the same interview, Macdonald is asked about the parallel trend of social-commentary comedy concerned with identity politics (e.g., Amy Schumer, Aziz Ansari), to which he replies:

"If you can tell me one funny, socially relevant joke I'd give you a million dollars. Comedians, when they get really good, and nowadays they don't even have to get good, reach a point where they feel they should be philosophers. I've heard it said even that the modern-day philosophers are comedians. I read modern-day philosophers! I'm sure they're insulted when they're compared to people who work in smoky nightclubs and hit on waitresses for a living" (Marchese, 2016).

He expressed great admiration for Preston Sturges' film *Sullivan's Travels*, the moral of which is that audiences don't want to be lectured to by entertainers who think they are smarter than the audience, but want pure comedy to escape their suffering and droll lives.[73]

---

[73] *Norm Macdonald Live*, August 29, 2017, https://vimeo.com/456848863.

In an interview a couple of years later, Macdonald expands upon this theme, discussing comedy as an art form[74] and pointing out the corrosive effects of postmodernism:

> "I guess there came a time, and I missed it, when revealing everything started to be considered art. I'd always learned that concealing everything was art. And I still believe that, because comedy is a vulgar art; it's an art that's just beginning to take form because it's so young. But I can look at other art forms and see how postmodernism has destroyed them, and now threatens to destroy stand-up… That's not to say that comedy can't make a greater point, because it can. But it can't make a greater point by screeching to a stop in the middle of the comedy show, making a point, and then going back to the jokes. You've got to craft the point into the joke. I always bristle when people say, 'The comedian is the modern-day philosopher.' There *are* modern-day philosophers" (Marchese, 2018).

In a follow-up question to Macdonald's thoughts on the nature of art and concealment, the interviewer asks him if his posts on Twitter are often about him trying to upset other people's expectations. "Which is why I sometimes feel like I'm considered right wing," Macdonald replies, "I'm just f*cking around" (Marchese, 2018).

Against Identity Politics

Right until the end, Macdonald's array of distinctly un-PC jokes drove libs crazy… for the most part, they hated him. In the unedited version of his 2011 special *Me Doing Standup*, his brutal "San Francisco" bit (which actually received a positive response before a San Francisco audience) is designed to lampoon the absurd girth which identity politics has taken on in contemporary society.[75]

---

[74] In some interviews, Macdonald expressed how he does *not* think of stand-up comedy as an art form but as a craft. "I think art means something that two different people can look at and see two different things. But with stand-up, it's all about getting that noise -- getting that laugh. And it has to come for everyone at the same time. Everyone has to think the same thing at the same time" (Marchese, 2016).

Macdonald opposed all forms of identity politics and seemed acutely aware of the double-standard, or more specifically the anti-white bias, that currently exists in our culture when it comes to matters of collective identity:

> "I hate that we force people into identifying themselves by little tiny... Because we oppress people, we further oppress them by forcing them to identify themselves as what I consider less-than-human. So, if someone says 'I am proud to be black,' I go 'That's too bad for that guy', because it's a retarded thing to be proud of. We see it with White Power. If someone says 'I'm proud to be white,' we see how ridiculous that sounds. But we don't see it when a person says, because they've been oppressed, 'I'm proud to be black,' but it *is* ridiculous. We've pushed them into a corner where now they're going to spend their whole life identifying themselves by the pigment of their skin, which is a sad waste of life" (MacPherson, 2012).

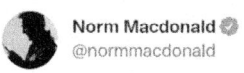

Norm Macdonald ✔
@normmacdonald

Where can I find all the new words out there, the crazy new words necessary to identify all the differences in people. Looking for a list of those words if you guys know where I can find one.

7:58 PM · Apr 29, 2019 · Twitter Web Client

To give an idea of just how fast woke terminology has permeated our culture, and what an early barometer Macdonald was, in his 2016 conversation with frequent Ricky Gervais collaborator Stephen Merchant (who in all likelihood is himself a liberal), Merchant has no idea what "cis male" means when Macdonald broaches the subject. "It's a way of marginalizing a normal person," Macdonald succinctly explains.[76]

---

[75] https://youtu.be/rlE8UAK3mMM
[76] *Norm Macdonald Live*, September 16, 2016,

He also dared to poke fun at the cultural obsession with 'white privilege'.[77] Replying to a since-deleted tweet by Nell Scovell – a Jewish comedy writer who is something of an activist against the comedy world's "white maleness" – Macdonald sarcastically replied:

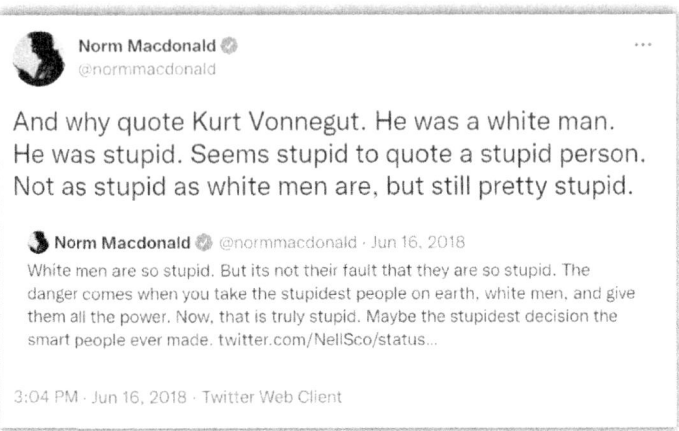

> **Norm Macdonald** ✓
> @normmacdonald   ...
>
> And why quote Kurt Vonnegut. He was a white man.
> He was stupid. Seems stupid to quote a stupid person.
> Not as stupid as white men are, but still pretty stupid.
>
> ▶ **Norm Macdonald** ✓ @normmacdonald · Jun 16, 2018
> White men are so stupid. But its not their fault that they are so stupid. The
> danger comes when you take the stupidest people on earth, white men, and give
> them all the power. Now, that is truly stupid. Maybe the stupidest decision the
> smart people ever made. twitter.com/NellSco/status...
>
> 3:04 PM · Jun 16, 2018 · Twitter Web Client

Jewish Jokes

Macdonald would occasionally foray into the un-forayable. A joke from his *Weekend Update* years:

> "Earlier this week, Marlon Brando met with Jewish leaders to apologize for comments he made on Larry King Live, among them that 'Hollywood is run by Jews.' The Jewish leaders accepted the actor's apology and announced that Brando is now free to work again."[78]

In another joke he did on *Weekend Update*, one wonders if he is just being provocative or is deliberately (and covertly) expressing the notion that, in rejecting Jesus Christ as Savior, Jews are condemned to damnation:

https://youtu.be/BHxmMbeZlAM.
[77] *Norm Macdonald Live*, August 22, 2017, https://youtu.be/dBoq3YeNH6o.
[78] *Saturday Night Live*, April 20, 1996.

"A group of Orthodox rabbis declared that other branches of Judaism are 'not Judaism at all,' thus challenging the religious status of millions of American Jews. This week, that statement was rejected by Reform leader Rabbi Don Schonstein, who said 'our legitimacy as Jews flows from the richness of our Jewish lives, the strength of our Jewish communities, and most important of all, our deep and abiding belief in Jesus Christ.'"[79]

On telephone dial-ins to *The Dennis Miller Show*, Macdonald would do bits pivoting around his faux "postmodern ventriloquism" act (where the act "cops to the fact that it's an inanimate object"). In these bits, Macdonald introduces his "virulently anti-Semitic" ventriloquist dummy Alec McGarrison who "doesn't believe the Holocaust happened." Describing Alec to Miller (who is doubled-over in laughter), Macdonald says:

"He's the worst. First of all, he's just plain wrong. He's not like an evil guy, he's just ignorant... I'm trying to get rid of that guy... He's an enthusiastic Holocaust denier, and I've had it up to *here* with that character. You know, man? It's just a waste of wood. But I don't know what to do. One of my Jewish friends suggested that, you know, why don't I just throw him on a fire and burn him. But I say two wrongs don't make a right."

Miller then asks Macdonald to bring Alec out and Macdonald abides. Macdonald then has a brief 'conversation' with Alec. When asked by Macdonald what he thinks about Christmas, Alec replies with an accusation of Jewish deicide: "I'm not gonna celebrate no holiday where a bunch of bearded New Yorkers killed our savior!".[80] At a later dial-in, Miller asks Macdonald if he still has the Holocaust-denying dummy and Macdonald answers: "It turned out he's wildly unsuccessful."

A repeating riff on *Norm Macdonald Live* involved Macdonald using his longtime friend and sidekick Adam Eget (who is Jewish) as a surrogate for introducing David Irving's Holocaust revisionism and

---

[79] *Saturday Night Live*, April 12, 1997.
[80] *The Dennis Miller Show*, https://youtu.be/I1c7_691tFQ.

for asking why other 20th century genocides (e.g., Stalin's Holodomor; the Armenian genocide by the Ottomans) are not as well-known as the Holocaust.[81] Macdonald would deploy a similar masking technique on *Norm Macdonald Live* when he'd have guests read bad, and often un-PC, jokes from blue cards, sometimes to the their dismay.[82]

His "4/20" bit[83] involved his sidekick Adam Egat reading a news story about the "4/20" cannabis-oriented, subcultural phenomenon in America, where people are celebrating "4/20", wearing "4/20" apparel, etc. Macdonald then turns to his laptop and pretends to read a Wikipedia entry about Adolf Hitler for the first time.

> "4/20 was the birthday of Austrian-born German politician, and the leader of the National Socialist German Workers Party, a fellow that went by the name of Adolf Hitler... But this guy -- there's a picture of him... a very compelling figure... odd-looking duck... But there's something about his eyes... hypnotic... His eyes are almost entirely black! He was a decorated veteran of World War I. Huh. And he joined the... hold the fort! He hated Jews. I'm sick of these characters. I think we should kill Hitler, me and you suicide, kill him."

When Eget tells him that Hitler already died, Macdonald replies: "Did he? I didn't even know he was sick," a line allusive to his own cancer. "I wish I could find the Hitler of today and go kill him," he ends the bit with, while staring directly at Eget.

Macdonald ends his last stand-up special *Hitler's Dog, Gossip and Trickery* (2017) with the show's eponymous joke:

---

[81] https://youtu.be/czWWjlSsylo. Macdonald confirms the Eget-as-surrogate angle in Rose (2021). At a 2016 book event in Washington D.C. for *Based on a True Story*, there's a funny but awkward moment when an audience member, commenting on Geoff Edgers' *Washington Post* profile of Macdonald earlier that year (titled "Will somebody please give Norm Macdonald another TV show?"), says: "If Norm Macdonald was a member of the Tribe, he'd be on TV."

[82] https://youtu.be/pIKlq1r6gdY.

[83] https://www.youtube.com/watch?v=jAzRb_lErFw.

Hitler had a dog. Now, you think of that. I'm no fan of Hitler. I never liked him. I didn't like him before it was cool not to like him.

But there was a dog in history who loved Hitler more than anyone. He would wake up in the morning and go, "Where's Hitler?!"
And Göring, or somebody, would go, "He's not here. He's doing some evil stuff... I've explained to you, he spends most of his time doing evil stuff. You can't see him that often."

[The dog] goes, "Okay. Yeah, I know... I'm not trying to... Listen, Göring, I love you, you know? I love Mengele, I love everybody. All you guys are the greatest. But it's just... *Hitler is the greatest man who's ever lived.*"

Macdonald waits a few beats and then adds:

This is why we ask that you don't use recording devices. I don't want to be with f*cking Harvey Levin tomorrow or something. "Did you say Hitler was the greatest?" And what would be my f*cking answer? I would go, "No, it was a dog." That wouldn't work. I would be f*cked.

But I'll be goddamned if I'm going to end a special talking about Hitler.

Yeah, that's what *I'm* going to do... End a special...

I'm going to call my special *Hitler's Dog.*

Macdonald would offset these types of jokes, and deflect charges of anti-Semitism, with material such as telling David Letterman "You know, with Hitler, the more I learn about that guy, the more I don't care for him," or his famous "Germany" bit which begins: "There *is* one country that worries me though — not Iran, not Iraq, not North Korea. The only country that really worries me is the country of Germany. I don't know if you guys are history buffs or not..."[84]

---

[84] *The Late Show with David Letterman*, May 15, 2015,

In his appearance on *Norm Macdonald Live*[85], while breaking down certain types of 'inside show-business' jokes, Jerry Seinfeld says to Macdonald that he (Jerry) will tell a joke that only Jews will get, and that Macdonald won't get. "The setup of the joke is it's a Jew joke," Seinfeld says. "Two Gentile businessmen meet on the street. One of them says 'How's business?' The other one says 'Great!'" Macdonald, in fact, doesn't laugh (or at least doesn't signal that he gets the joke). Seinfeld adds that "The joke is about who doesn't get it. That's part of what makes the joke funny." In the Jewish publication *The Forward*, a staff-written eulogy in memory of Macdonald takes for granted this particular form of ethnocentric consciousness, but in the process may reveal some of Macdonald's own deeply-closeted ethnocentric consciousness:

> Seinfeld has just finished a long explanation of how gentiles often miss Jewish humor. He illustrates it by telling a classic Jewish joke (funny) that he promises Macdonald won't understand. Macdonald, indeed, doesn't get it (funnier). Then, later, as the show wraps, Seinfeld asks Macdonald if he makes any money doing the show. Macdonald says he doesn't think so. Seinfeld can't believe a comedian would show up anywhere for free. Macdonald shrugs, "Ah, gentile." (Funniest).[86]

#MeToo Controversy

Macdonald openly criticized the guilty-before-proven-innocent #MeToo movement, which got him pulled into the cancel culture vortex. When asked about this by an obnoxiously leftist interviewer, he replies:

> "I'm happy the #MeToo movement has slowed down a little bit. It used to be, 'One hundred women can't be lying.' And then it became, 'One woman can't lie.' And that became, 'I believe all women.' And then you're like, 'What?'" (Abramovitch, 2018)

https://youtu.be/mFjEvl43zYY?t=300.

[85] *Norm Macdonald Live*, August 29, 2017, https://vimeo.com/456848863.

[86] "Norm Macdonald's gift to Jewish humor," *The Forward*, September 14, 2021.

In our increasingly woke and unforgiving cancel culture, Macdonald lamented the waning role of forgiveness. "What about when someone admits to wrongdoing?" the interviewer asks him, to which he replies:

> "The model used to be: admit wrongdoing, show complete contrition and then we give you a second chance. Now it's admit wrongdoing and you're finished. And so the only way to survive is to deny, deny, deny. That's not healthy — that there is no forgiveness" (Abramovitch, 2018).

When he is then asked about Roseanne Barr's 2018 firing from the *Roseanne* reboot (for tweets that she quickly renounced publicly and apologized for), Macdonald replies with noticeable contempt towards the reporter:

> "I feel bad that Roseanne got fired. I think we have to be more forgiving of people. I've spoken to Roseanne many times. She's always been in tears. She's paying a mighty penance for whatever transgression *you* might think she did" (Abramovitch, 2018).[87]

Macdonald's defense of Roseanne and Louis C.K. – despite his own subsequent clarification of this defense -- led to a scheduled appearance on Jimmy Fallon's show being cancelled, as some woke Fallon staff members were literally crying at the idea that Macdonald would appear.

Appearing on Howard Stern's radio show, Macdonald apologized for his comments, but his apology was compounded when, as he explains it, he was about to use the word "retarded" to mean dumb (as people of his generation often use the word), but instantaneously switched to the word "Down Syndrome" instead.[88]

---

[87] Macdonald's defense of Barr and Louis C.K. – despite his own subsequent recanting of this defense -- led to a scheduled appearance on Jimmy Fallon's show being cancelled.

[88] The context was in Macdonald saying "You'd have to have Down syndrome to not feel sorry" for victims of sexual abuse. (*Howard Stern Show*, September 12, 2018).

Roseanne and Louis have both been very good friends of mine for many years. They both made terrible mistakes and I would never defend their actions. If my words sounded like I was minimizing the pain that their victims feel to this day, I am deeply sorry.

7:47 PM · Sep 11, 2018 · Twitter Web Client

In a further act of socially-sanctioned contrition, he then appeared on *The View* the next day to clarify all of these accumulated comments.[89] However, it did not prevent his Netflix show *Norm Macdonald Has a Show* from not being renewed for a second season.

Male Humor

After his death, liberals began pointing out "problematic" aspects of Macdonald's character and material, with accusations of misogyny, 'attacks' on women, homophobia and the like.[90] Macdonald's fanbase was substantially more male than female, and his traditionalist attitudes regarding gender comes through clearly in his material, much to the chagrin of progressives.

For instance, in a 2018 interview, Macdonald briefly critiqued Hannah Gadsby, the insufferably woke, mentally ill, lesbian

---

[89] *The View*, September 13, 2018, https://youtu.be/eH7QgHs3ZrE.

[90] One of the offended is Nancy Norton, a comedian and plural-pronoun-person. The twisted contortions applied to the English language in this *The Daily Beast* article (Roundtree, 2021) are cringeworthy:

> 'Norton tells *The Daily Beast* that Macdonald trying to reduce them on stage after they had such a successful set made them feel "like shit." So, when Norton finally saw Macdonald again a few years later, they approached him about the comment and said how uncomfortable it made them feel… Norton says they grappled with whether to post their story, because they don't necessarily agree with "cancel culture," but think there should be a dialogue opened up'.

performer of finger-wagging, lecturing 'confessional comedy', simply saying:

> "I have never seen the *Nanette* thing because I never wanted to comment on it. But from what I have read about it, [Gadsby] is saying that comedy is now not about laughter. And of course that's a slap in the face of a traditional stand-up comedian who thinks that comedy by dictionary definition is about laughter... *Nanette* doesn't sound like stand-up to me. That sounds like a one-woman show. And one-person shows are, to me, incredibly powerful. But it's not stand-up comedy and it's not the same thing" (Abramovitch, 2018).

The same day this interview posted, Gadsby tweeted the following:

Hannah Gadsby ✔
@Hannahgadsby

I'd never heard of this Norm McDonald bloke because I didn't want to make a comment about him. I don't like him though. #dickbiscuit

7:39 PM · Sep 11, 2018 · Twitter Web Client

Indirectly, Macdonald was critical of the feminization of culture. For example, in one radio interview, after describing the occupation of teaching as incredibly easy (e.g., summers off; dealing only with children; union protection), which he adds he witnessed in his youth (given both of his parents were teachers), he then mocks the oft-cited characterization of moms and teachers as "heroes", sarcastically saying: "The *real* heroes are the moms and the teachers, not the guys on Iwo Jima planting the flag. Not the firemen who run into buildings. No, no, no... it's the teacher! It's a person that shows up at a school... as the tallest person in the class."[91]

"Male humor prefers the laugh to be at someone's expense," wrote Christopher Hitchens, "and understands that life is quite possibly a joke to begin with -- and often a joke in extremely poor

---

[91] *The Sarah & Vinnie Show*, Interview with Norm Macdonald, September 23, 2008, https://youtu.be/zSQj2HIpA7Y?t=402.

taste" (Hitchens, 2007). That men have dominated stand-up comedy since its inception may have as much to do with returning to the childishness of male youth as it has to do with contemporary observational content. "When people come to see me do stand-up," Macdonald writes in *Based on a True Story*, "it is because somewhere in their memory I live on SNL… They tell me they are big fans and they don't care what their girlfriends say."

Religion

Macdonald was raised Presbyterian[92] and was a Christian most of his life, with varying degrees of commitment. There were some detours, but Christianity was the primary theological vehicle for a lifelong spiritual journey that took him into different directions. One can speculate that since his earliest diagnosis of cancer (which would go back to at least 1991 and possibly earlier), he more deeply explored existentialist literature and philosophy. In grappling with existential dread, he seems to have read across the spectrum of both theology and secularism, wavering in his faith from time to time, and always engaging in profanity, but in the end reconnecting with Christianity not through any denomination but through a private faith.

In a stand-up set from 2009, for example, he articulates a form of Pascal's Wager: "There's solely two issues. You've obtained to take a look at the proof that God exists. None. That's not good. Then you go, 'What's the proof God doesn't exist?' None. So they're equal. One of them is for certain proper" (Walther, 2021). Later in life, he became a bit more outspoken about his Christianity, but was still visibly uncomfortable discussing the subject. When asked by Larry King if he's a religious believer, Macdonald replies: "I'm a Christian. It's not stylish to say that now." From this same interview, we learn that he was cognizant of the Kierkegaardian leap of faith his belief required. When King then asks him if he believes he's going somewhere when life ends, Macdonald replies: "Well, I don't *believe* it... What people don't understand about faith is that you have to *choose*. You know what I mean? They think that you believe it -- but you have to choose."[93]

In a 2011 interview where he touched upon a range of topics, including mortality and his quest to strengthen his faith, Macdonald

---

[92] See Edgers, "Norm Macdonald Book Tour" interview, 2016.
[93] *Larry King Now*, October 17, 2016, https://youtu.be/7kbBIWnVjpA.

said: "What I'm trying to get to is God… I read lots of literature -- Tolstoy, Faulkner -- and faith keeps coming up… Why are all these guys… it all comes down to faith, you know? It seems like every great f*cking novel I read, it seems like faith is the only salvation" (Maron, 2011).

Of the God Hypothesis in general, he believed it was wrong to limit ones approach to it with empirical standards. "They're thinking of it in evidentiary ways," he said in an interview, "There is an enormous intuition -- amongst every person who has ever lived -- that God exists" (MacPherson, 2012).

In 2015, as a judge on *Last Comic Standing*, he sternly rebuked an anti-Christian comic.[94] This comic – a Jewish homosexual from NYC – told a joke which involved his complaining about people quoting Biblical chapter & verse to him on the subway. The joke's punchline involves him giving the Christian offender a counter-quote:

> "If you're going to quote from *your* favorite book, I should be able to quote from *my* favorite book. He was like 'Men do not live on bread alone: Matthew 4:4'… I was like 'Everybody's a little bit magic: Harry Potter, Chapter 7'. Not a fair fight, right? One of those books is a classic about a man who has sacrificed himself for the good of the world. And the other is the Bible."

When it came his turn to critique this comic, Macdonald's face is dour as he tells him:

> "I don't think the Bible joke was brave at all. I think if you're going to take on an entire religion, you should maybe know what you're talking about. J.K. Rowling is a Christian, and J.K. Rowling famously said that if you're familiar with the scriptures, you could easily guess the ending of her book."

There were hints of his theological investment. For instance, during his conversation with Jane Fonda, Macdonald asks her "Are you a religious person?" She replies "I have faith," to which Macdonald inquires "In Jesus Christ?" Fonda pauses and then says "I'm still a work in progress. I believe in the historical Jesus."

---

[94] https://youtu.be/kG7xj76_-dY

Macdonald follows up by asking her "Would you believe in the hypostatic Jesus?" Fonda says "no," and Macdonald replies, "So, you're not a Christian. But you believe… you believe in *something*."[95]

At one point, Macdonald explored Judaism and had regular discussions with rabbis, believing Judaism would lead him towards a fuller understanding of the Old Testament. "I don't like organized religion so much. I know two rabbis and I talk to them a lot because I don't understand the Old Testament and they do. They know stuff. I was raised Protestant and they don't know anything" (Marchese, 2018). He once stated that he "became Jewish" for two years.

In his most extensive and expansive interview on philosophical and religious topics, Macdonald rhetorically argues an anti-natalist position against Richard Dawkins; discusses the problem of evil; says he is of no specific faith (but is closer to Judaism than anything else); and in the face of existential dread rejects the idea that man can, without God, create his own purpose and meaning (MacPherson, 2012).

In November 2018, he wrote a rather weighty Counter-Enlightenment tweet which he would delete just days later:

Norm Macdonald ✓ @normmacd… · 12h ∨
The Enlightenment turned us away from truth and toward a darkling weakening horizon, sad and grey to see. The afterglow of Christianity is near gone now, and a stygian silence lurks in wait.

As time went on, Macdonald became increasingly vocal in his rejection of cynicism, choosing instead to view the wondrous aspects of life as Blakean manifestations of godly enchantment. Two tweets from 2018:

---

[95] *Norm Macdonald Has a Show*, September 14, 2018. The concept of the hypostatic Jesus is that the two 'sides' of Jesus – the human and the divine – are united in one God-man.

> **Norm Macdonald** ✓
> @normmacdonald   ...
>
> The idiot sees the world as Good vs Evil. The cynic
> sees the world as Evil vs Evil. The truth that no one
> seems able to see is that the world is, and always has
> been, a battle of Good vs. Good.
>
> 5:50 PM · Jun 25, 2018 · Twitter Web Client

> **Norm Macdonald** ✓
> @normmacdonald   ...
>
> At times, the joy that life attacks me with is unbearable
> and leads to gasping hysterical laughter. I find myself
> completely out of control and wonder how could life
> could surprise me again and again and again, so
> completely. How could a man be a cynic? It is a sin.
>
> 3:08 AM · Apr 17, 2018 · Twitter Web Client

Matthew Walther is correct in describing Macdonald as a "considerably idiosyncratic Christian comic" whose comedy was "remarkably freed from malice, and lately it was marked by startling shows of mercy and humility" (Walther, 2021).[96]

Themes of generosity, kindness, compassion and love began to preoccupy him in his last years. In 2018, with his friend and entrepreneur Vivek Jain, Macdonald co-founded a video dating app called Loko. Macdonald's involvement in this venture, something atypical for him, appears to have been motivated by his dislike of the effect apps such as Tinder are having in fostering transactional sexual relationships among younger generations:

> "Well, I feel like a super old man trying to save the world from debauchery," Macdonald says, alluding to other apps that have a reputation for users seeking hook-ups instead of dates. "I think we both want to try to bring a little romance back to life. My god, it can't go much further the other way. I always think when my buddies tell me all these stories with

---

[96] See also Rowan (2021)

girls, I go, 'The world hasn't changed that much since I knew girls.' I don't think these other apps are what people want in life" (Hahn, 2020)[97]

A tweet from 2019 reads:

Norm Macdonald ✔ @normmacdonald · Apr 10, 2019
Neil, there is a logic flaw in your little aphorism that seems quite telling. Since you and I are part of the Universe, then we would also be indifferent and uncaring. Perhaps you forgot, Neil, that we are not superior to the Universe but merely a fraction of it. Nice day, indeed

Neil deGrasse Tyson ✔ @neiltyson · Apr 3, 2019
The Universe is blind to our sorrows and indifferent to our pains.

Have a nice day!

"Remember," he tweeted in 2020, "without compassion there can exist no morality."[98] In a 2018 interview, he outlined where he hoped his third act of material would go, thematically. He talked about wanting to do material about God and love, in a way that had not yet been done in stand-up comedy.

> "[T]he two themes I'm interested in now are God and love. That's the hardest stuff to write about in a comedic way. It's so easy to write about the pain or the ordinariness of man. It's not that I have a great deal of jokes right now about love and God, but I thought those would be, by far, the hardest subjects and that that [material] would be part of my third special and then I'd be finished… with comedy entirely. I don't have that much to say" (Marchese, 2018).

Towards the end of *Based on a True Story*, reflecting on his journey from laborer to celebrity comedian, Macdonald writes:

---

[97] When asked if he uses Loko himself, Macdonald replied: "God no, I'm an old man. I'm just an old chunk of coal. I don't even know how to use my phone" (Siegler, 2018).

[98] https://twitter.com/normmacdonald/status/1315085010483859457

Before I was famous I had a whole bunch of jobs where all I needed was boots. People would look right past me, or if they did look at me, it was with a *mean* look. But when I got famous, people would look at me and smile and wonder where they knew me from. If they flat-out recognized me, they'd laugh and dance like they'd won a prize, and I'd just stand there and smile and feel warmth from their love. So the fame made the world, which is a real cold place, a little less cold.

For Macdonald the chronic gambler, perhaps the theological positions he ultimately settled upon were a Pascal's Wager means of dealing with his own illness and the existential horror of mortality, an extended variation of the 'deathbed conversion' theme. And, as many others have noticed, the subject of death has long been a preoccupation for him, finding its way into his material in unique and novel ways.

EIGHT

Death

Upon Macdonald's death, we can look in the rearview mirror and contextualize the air of melancholy and the degree of gallows humor that surfaced in both his material and interviews. The subject of death was in his material for most of his professional career, but in his later years, commensurate with the timeline of his own terminal illness, he would increasingly broach the topic, tackling everything from heart attacks and illness to suicide.[99]

As previously noted, Macdonald experienced stomach cancer as early as 1986 when he was still in his twenties, and possibly earlier (Brownstein, 1991). In a 1995 follow-up column on Macdonald by the same reporter, the stomach cancer has changed to "gastro-intestinal disorder", an early indication that Macdonald wanted to keep his cancer a secret (Brownstein, 1995). The trauma that these cancer experiences likely had on his psyche, leading him to obsess with the issue of mortality and its inevitability, is understandable. When cancer struck him again circa 2012, he would keep this condition hidden from all but his closest friends and family.

"I can't stop myself from constantly ruminating over death" he told Marc Maron in 2011. Macdonald was continuously trying to weave the subject into his routines, and believed he'd only been successful to a limited degree. "I took away a lot more of my existential brooding on death that I haven't really figured out yet. It leaves people a little sad. I have to figure out a way to work on that" (Itzfoff, 2011). Macdonald was greatly influenced by Ernest Becker's 1974 book *The Denial of Death*, and saw obsessing over one's mortality a sign of "indulgence". He deduced that it was irrational to spend an inordinate amount of time "ruminating about an inevitability," yet his death anxiety (thanatophobia) was such that he could not stop himself from doing so. He further voiced an Epicurean argument on

---

[99] See for instance *Hitler's Dog, Gossip and Trickery* (2017), https://www.youtube.com/watch?v=Sh7QWBb2U2A.

the nature of death by saying: "Since when you're dead, you're not alive… and since when you're alive, you're not dead… you and death will never actually cross paths, so there's really nothing to be afraid of" (MacPherson, 2012). Regarding one's fear of no longer existing, Macdonald recounts in an interview with Larry King how Nabokov, upon seeing a family photo representing a moment in time before he himself was born (the photo depicted his mother and siblings), felt no fear or terror, even though he was looking at a picture of a time when he didn't exist. Nabokov concluded, qua the Ancient Roman philosopher Lucretius, that we should therefore not fear death, which is future time when one no longer exists.[100]

Macdonald begins *Based on a True Story* with a true anecdote from 2013 (which would have been within the first year of his leukemia diagnosis) where his agent called him and told him "You're dead… Check your Wikipedia page."[101] The 'Norm Macdonald' character of the book heads over to his laptop:

> Over at the table I hit a couple of buttons on my computer and discover what my agent found so funny. Some joker has changed my Wikipedia page, all right, and he's left me for dead. "Norm Macdonald (October 17, 1963–May 12, 2013) was a comedian and actor who was known from…" I read on and on till the final sentence. The death sentence. "Mr. Macdonald was found dead in an Edmonton hotel room from an overdose of morphine."

This incident, he has said, was a key motivation for him to begin working on the book, although we now know that this motivation was of course greatly amplified by his leukemia diagnosis. Although

---

[100] *Larry King Now* (October 17, 2016). https://youtu.be/7kbBIWnVjpA?t=370. Lucretius wrote: "Look back at time… before our birth. In this way Nature holds before our eyes the mirror of our future after death. Is this so grim, so gloomy?" (Lucretius, 1951.)

[101] This anecdote is even more eerie when, if we are to believe Macdonald, he was staying at the very same Edmonton hotel room at the time. "One time I was in a hotel room in Edmonton, Canada and my manager called and told me that on my Wikipedia (page), it said I was dead and I looked on Wikipedia and sure enough, someone had changed my Wikipedia and said that I had died of a morphine overdose in the very hotel room I was standing in… Reading my obituary… it sounded very chilling. Even though it was a joke" (*New York Daily News*, 2016).

Macdonald did not discuss his cancer publicly, he would brush against the topic indirectly, through fictional surrogates in his stand-up comedy and abstractly in interviews. He comes closest to revealing his cancer while being interviewed by Larry King.[102] On the topic of death, there is an exchange between them which may indicate that Macdonald explored end-of-life options. King poses a rhetorical question:

> KING: "When you slept last night, you could've been dead. So, if you didn't wake up this morning, how would you know?"
>
> NORM: "Well, that's true, sir. You know, I've been looking into this... Nowadays -- my doctor tells me -- they can put you to sleep... and you go to sleep. And two weeks later, you don't wake up... your heart stops. But you can go to sleep for two weeks, and not have to endure howling anguish and pain."
>
> KING: "No cancer, no nothing..."
>
> NORM: "It's all gone."

The brief nervous laugh that Macdonald then expresses, perhaps thinking he has revealed too much, speaks volumes.

In a 2016 interview with Chris Hardwick, Macdonald articulates his disdain for confessional comedy being interpreted as 'courageous', and as a contrast discusses the suicide of character actor Richard Farnsworth, who had cancer. "He was nominated for an Academy Award for [*The Straight Story*]," Macdonald notes, "and if he had said he was filled with cancer, he would have won, for sure. But, instead, he *didn't* say it, and in fact *no one* knew it. His family didn't know it; he kept it from everyone." Macdonald then characterizes Farnsworth's suicide in a way that deviates from Christian orthodoxy: "*That* to me is courageous. You're not being a burden to your family, they know nothing about it, and then you're gone... He wrote a nice letter to everybody in the family and said the reason he did it is he didn't want to cause people to stress."[103]

---

[102] *Larry King Now* (October 17, 2016), https://youtu.be/7kbBIWnVjpA?t=335

Macdonald opens his mercifully short-lived *Back to Norm* (2005) sketch comedy show with a particularly dark and macabre parody of Bud Dwyer's televised suicide in 1987, but this time it involved 'Norm Macdonald' reading a brief statement to the press before the act:

> "My name is Norm Macdonald and when I became a comedian all I ever wanted to do was make people laugh, and perhaps make them think as well. However, I've come to realize that failure has dogged me at every turn, and that mediocrity has been my hallmark. So it is with a heavy heart, but a clear conscience, [that] I've decided to retire from show business."[104]

Later in the Las Vegas exploits of *Based on a True Story*, the 'Norm' character plots a harebrained and all-but-certain-to-fail Vegas gambling scheme which he calls 'Plan A'. Should this scheme fail, 'Norm' will then initiate 'Plan B', which involves committing suicide via a lethal dose of Dilaudid (an opioid).[105] The gambling scheme fails, of course, and 'Norm' retreats to his hotel room:

> I sit on the edge of my bed and open the drawer. I take out the 600 milligrams of Dilaudid, the fresh syrette, and the Gideon's Bible. I read a few of my favorite Scripture passages as I prepare the syrettes. And then I inject myself with the lethal dose of Dilaudid. I fall to my knees and rest my elbows on the bed. I pray forgiveness for what I am doing. And then I feel joy and peace fill my soul as my consciousness quietly drifts away.

In the novel, 'Norm' does not die but instead meets God, in a very funny interlude involving God choosing a Dilaudid-stoned Norm to write down God's new message for humanity. ("Now, people always wonder if God is a man or a woman or black or white

---

[103] *The Nerdist Podcast*, Interview with Norm Macdonald, October 12, 2016, https://youtu.be/7unyDYKgap0.

[104] *Back to Norm*, Comedy Central, May 29, 2005, https://youtu.be/wquzFdug5y0.

[105] Does this scene from the book indicate that Macdonald considered doing this himself (as his comments on *Larry King Now* would seem to indicate) or is it a playful riff on the strange and unsettling Wikipedia incident? Or might it be both?

or yellow," Norm says, "but I'm here to tell you that none of this silly stuff matters. He's a white guy, by the way.")

In his stand-up routines, Macdonald's delivery is integral to the effectiveness of his more morbid material. "My dad died, and my grandfather died, and my great-grandfather died. And the guy before him, I don't know… probably died," he says in *Me Doing Standup* (2011). "I come from a long line of death." In that same stand-up special he says "You ever be having a really good dream, and then, right in the middle of the dream, you wake up… right in the best part of the dream? And there you are, back in your stinkin' life again? Man, that's rough, eh?" He has a riff about heart attacks in this special as well: "What's the odds that a terrorist will attack and kill you? Almost zero. But what are the odds you'll be attacked and killed by your own heart? It's about a 100%." On *Norm Macdonald Has a Show*, he says to Drew Barrymore "When I die, I want all my friends to gather around," holding a long pause, "and try to bring me back to life!"

As noted above, Macdonald found it absurd how we frame someone dying from cancer as a 'courageous battle', embroidering a brute fact of existence and mortality with a misplaced attribution of heroics: "In the old days," goes one of his bits, "they'd go, 'Hey, that old man died.'… Now they go, 'Hey, he lost his battle'… I'm pretty sure if *you* die, the cancer also dies at exactly the same time. So that, to me, is not a loss… that's a draw." (Macdonald, 2011).[106] In this same extended bit, he draws upon a fictionalized uncle to discuss something he himself likely experienced. "So, My Uncle Bert is 'waging a courageous battle', which I've seen because I go and visit him, and this is the battle: he's lying in a hospital bed with a thing in his arm, watching *Matlock* on the TV."[107]

At the same time, Macdonald could write beautiful, somber meditations on the fleeting nature of youth and the certainty of mortality: "The only thing an old man can tell a young man is that it goes fast, real fast, and if you're not careful it's too late. Of course, the young man will never understand this truth" (*Based on a True Story*,

---

[106] https://youtu.be/NMRd-n_s4c8

[107] In the bit, 'Uncle Bert' is suffering from stomach cancer. Macdonald's brother has stated that there is no Uncle Bert (Neil Macdonald, 2016). It's also worth noting that, in *Based on a True Story*, Macdonald references the show *Matlock*, which featured Andy Griffith as a lawyer, several times. "I had seen every single episode of *Matlock* many times over," the 'Norm' character says at one point.

p. 230). Facing his own cancer sentence, his stoic philosophy precluded him from directly weaving his own condition into his material, and he viewed putting such experiences into a comedy act as unnecessary emotional baggage done in poor taste, and a sign of narcissism. "I've heard people go onstage and talk about cancer or some shit, and I go, 'Isn't this what happens to everybody?' They seem to think they're singular in their story when their story is the most common story that could possibly be, which is suffering and pain" (Marchese, 2018).

Instead, Macdonald would use surrogates. In the aforementioned section about the terminally ill boy in *Based on a True Story*, he writes:

> Death is a funny thing. Not funny haha, like a Woody Allen movie, but funny strange, like a Woody Allen marriage. When it's unexpected, death comes fast like a ravenous wolf and tears open your throat with a merciful fury. But when it's expected, it comes slow and patient like a snake, and the doctor tells you how far away it is and when, exactly, it will be at your door. And when it will be at the foot of your bed. And when it will be on your flesh. It's all right there on their clipboards.

In the online version of Geoff Edgers very insightful 2016 *Washington Post* profile of Macdonald, a sidebar contains a series of text messages between Edgers and Macdonald.[108] In one exchange, Macdonald asks Edgers: "Did you ever read the story about the fellow who bought an overcoat and it changed his entire life?" Edgers replies that he hasn't. In a lengthy series of texts that follows, Macdonald recounts the story contemporaneously, akin to his extended setup to the Moth Joke:

> Well, there was this fellow, you understand, who held a job in the government. It was a job that would not be missed if it was to be made redundant. And the man knew it. He was a paper-pusher, as they say. In the office where he worked, he worked alone. His job did not intersect with any of his colleagues. He was the type of man with the type of job that

---

[108] Macdonald gave Edgers permission to publish these private texts (Edgers, 2021).

men like you me, Geoff, should keep in mind whenever the hyenas of self-pity circle and approach.

The fellow was not laughed at, nothing like that. He was just ignored. Who knows which is worse. But he sat and he worked and was not noticed or greeted from 9 until 5.

There is a Christmas party approaching and the man becomes sad, as he does every Christmas party, because he knows he will be at the office, alone with the others, without work to distract him from the thought of this fact.

The day before the party he trudged through the grey streets and the wet snow is on his face and he looks on a shop window and sees an overcoat. He is [a] frugal man and not well paid but he decides entering the store to get a closer look [sic] will cost him nothing so he enters and takes a closer look at the overcoat. The salesman pays him much attention which only serves to make the man sad, of course. He tries on the overcoat. When he puts it on the salesman says how wonderful it looks, how it appears to have been made for the man himself. The other salesman [sic] all agree but the man has lived a loveless life and cynicism has hardened him to the compliments of sales folk. But he had to admit that his image in the mirror looked quite nice. And, then, other customers began to say how good the man looked, and the man was bewildered, and in an impulse bough [sic] the overcoat.

He wore the overcoat to the Christmas party. Everyone at the party was charmed by the overcoat and by the man who wore it. Secretaries flirted with him, colleagues asked him questions and planned drinks at a local bar and the boss even asked him to join him for golf. It was the finest the man had felt since he was a child and he walked home with a smile on his face and talked to himself, replaying different conversations he'd had during the party.

A gang of never-do/wells spotted and attacked him. They beat him up badly but worst of all they stole the overcoat.

89

The man fell into a snowbank and allowed himself to cry.

The end.

That was the first story I read when I was a kid. It's called The Overcoat, written by Gogol.

Unlike with the Moth Joke, there is no punchline here, just bleakness. Philosophically, Macdonald fixated on this type of existential fatalism, and struggled to find coherent religious ways to escape its clutches. But he also sought to assuage people of this existentialist dread through transitory moments of laughter and joy. "All my life's about is cracking up people and them cracking me up and trying not to think about dying," he's attributed with saying. "That doesn't cost very much money."[109]

Northrop Frye once wrote that "the theme of the comic is the integration of society," and among his fan base Macdonald served as a temporary harbor from which to try to make sense of, and integrate, both the postmodern cultural madness that has enveloped culture and the ineluctable fate that awaits us all.

In dying, Norm Macdonald in a strange sort of way gave us one last joke, perhaps the purest joke of all, where the setup and the punchline are nearly the same: the existential absurdity of existence and the complete unknowability of non-existence.

---

[109] https://www.brainyquote.com/quotes/norm_macdonald_557258

Works Cited

- Abramovitch, Seth. "Norm Macdonald Won't Go Pundit on His Netflix Talk Show," *The Hollywood Reporter*, September 11, 2018, https://www.hollywoodreporter.com/news/general-news/why-norm-macdonalds-new-talk-show-wont-target-trump-1141832/.
- Andrelczyk, Mike. "Remembering the Dark, Absurd Comedy of Norm Macdonald," *Lancaster Online*, October 10, 2021, https://lancasteronline.com/features/entertainment/remembering-the-dark-absurd-comedy-of-norm-macdonald-unscripted/article_8512d840-2861-11ec-849a-a3d37cb78124.html.
- Belz, Aaron. "Goodbye, Norm Macdonald," *Front Porch Republic*, September 16, 2021, https://www.frontporchrepublic.com/2021/09/goodbye-norm-macdonald/.
- Brooks, Dan. "Norm Macdonald, Still in Search of the Perfect Joke," *New York Times*, August 30, 2018, https://www.nytimes.com/2018/08/30/magazine/norm-macdonald-still-in-search-of-the-perfect-joke.html
- Brownstein, Bill. "Comedy Spotlight Leads Ottawa Native Macdonald to L.A.," *Montreal Gazette*, May 4, 1991, https://www.reddit.com/r/NormMacdonald/comments/q3usms/norms_first_bout_w_cancer_91_article_from/.
- Brownstein, Bill. "Ottawa-raised Norm Macdonald is deadpan delight off stage, too," *Montreal Gazette*, July 27, 1995, https://i.imgur.com/KEAAMNM.jpg
- Brownstein, Bill. "Before he was a household name, Norm Macdonald was a JFL smash," *Montreal Gazette*, September 14, 2021.
- Capshaw, Ron. "Norm Macdonald Is Conservative And Brave, A Rarity Among Comedians," *The Federalist*, September 14, 2018, https://thefederalist.com/2018/09/14/norm-macdonald-is-conservative-and-brave-a-rarity-among-comedians/.
- CBC News. "Comedian and actor Norm Macdonald dead at 61," CBC News, September 14, 2021,

https://www.cbc.ca/news/entertainment/norm-macdonald-dies-1.6175474.

- Chow, Andrew. "Norm Macdonald's Comedic Genius Explained in One Brilliant Joke," *Time*, September 15, 2021, https://time.com/6098035/norm-macdonald-comedy/.
- Diamond, Jonny. "The time Norm Macdonald dunked on Bret Easton Ellis in defense of Alice Munro," *Literary Hub*, September 15, 2021, https://lithub.com/the-time-norm-macdonald-dunked-on-bret-easton-ellis-in-defense-of-alice-munro/.
- Domenech, Ben. "There Will Never Be Another Norm Macdonald," *The Federalist*, September 15, 2021, https://thefederalist.com/2021/09/15/there-will-never-be-another-norm-macdonald/.
- Duignan-Cabrera, Anthony. "It's Why They're Called Punch Lines: Comedy: Norm MacDonald is known for landing hard ones on 'Saturday Night Live,' with O.J. and Bob Dole among his favorite targets," *Los Angeles Times*, December 23, 1995, https://www.latimes.com/archives/la-xpm-1995-12-23-ca-17179-story.html.
- Edgers, Geoff. "Will somebody please give Norm Macdonald another TV show?" *Washington Post*, August 18, 2016, https://www.washingtonpost.com/graphics/entertainment/norm-macdonald/.
- Edgers, Geoff. "Norm Macdonald Book Tour" [Interview with Norm Macdonald], Sixth & I Historic Synagogue, Washington D.C., September 22, 2016, https://youtu.be/oU81p6RN6b8.
- Edgers, Geoff. "Norm Macdonald was Tolstoy in sweatpants. Even when he texted you in the middle of the night," *Washington Post*, September 15, 2021, https://www.washingtonpost.com/entertainment/norm-macdonald-appreciation/2021/09/15/315f6f52-15eb-11ec-b976-f4a43b740aeb_story.html.
- Edgers, Geoff. "Remembering Norm Macdonald," *WBUR*, September 17, 2021, https://www.wbur.org/hereandnow/2021/09/17/remembering-norm-macdonald.
- Evans, Greg. "Norm Macdonald Dies: Influential Comedian & Former 'SNL' Weekend Update Anchor Was 61," *Deadline*, September 14, 2021, https://deadline.com/2021/09/norm-

macdonald-dead-obituary-comedian-saturday-night-live-weekend-update-anchor-was-61-1234833212/.

- Forward, The. "Norm Macdonald's gift to Jewish humor," *The Forward*, September 14, 2021, https://forward.com/fast-forward/475532/norm-macdonalds-gift-to-jewish-humor/.
- Frye, Northrop. *Anatomy of Criticism: Four Essays* (Princeton University Press, 1957).
- Gabriel, Jon. "Norm Macdonald: Dostoyevsky in Front of a Red Brick Wall," *Ricochet*, September 14, 2021, https://ricochet.com/1049936/norm-macdonald-dostoyevsky-in-front-of-a-red-brick-wall/.
- Gheciu, Alex Nino. "Norm Macdonald Is the Funniest Man (Not) on TV," *Sharp Magazine*, December 2, 2016, https://sharpmagazine.com/2016/12/02/norm-macdonald-is-the-funniest-man-not-on-tv/.
- Giovannone, Aaron. "The Anti-Politics and Anti-Comedy of Norm Macdonald," *Jacobin*, October 2021, https://www.jacobinmag.com/2021/10/norm-macdonald-anti-politics-anti-comedy-snl-subversion-stand-up.
- Gladwell, Malcolm. "How does a comedy outsider make sense of Norm Macdonald?", *Malcolm Gladwell Bulletin*, September 24, 2021, https://malcolmgladwell.bulletin.com/224534839714566/.
- Gordon, Doug. "Menefreghismo" (Interview with Norm Macdonald), May 07, 2017, https://www.ttbook.org/interview/menefreghismo.
- Grignan, Denis. "Former Gloucester High grad turns yuks into bucks," Orleans Magazine, May 1991, https://www.reddit.com/r/NormMacdonald/comments/q3vhiq/a_young_chunk_of_coal_in_orleans_magazine_1991_he/.
- Hahn, Jason Duaine. "You Could Meet Your Valentine on This Video-Only Dating App Created by Comedian Norm Macdonald," *People*, February 14, 2020, https://people.com/human-interest/you-could-meet-valentine-video-dating-app-created-norm-macdonald/.
- Harvilla, Rob. "Norm Macdonald Was an Agent of Comedy Chaos," *The Ringer*, September 14, 2021, https://www.theringer.com/tv/2021/9/14/22674425/norm-macdonald-obituary.

- Heisler, Steve. "Interview: Norm Macdonald," *A.V. Club*, April 12, 2011, https://www.avclub.com/norm-macdonald-1798225024.
- Hitchens, Christopher. "Why Women Aren't Funny," *Vanity Fair*, January 2007, https://www.vanityfair.com/culture/2007/01/hitchens200701.
- Hochman, Nate. "Norm Macdonald, Christian Comic," *National Review*, September 22, 2021, https://www.nationalreview.com/corner/norm-macdonald-christian-comic/.
- Horton, Kaleb. "The True Story of Norm Macdonald, Comedy's Best Liar," *Rolling Stone*, September 15, 2021, https://www.rollingstone.com/tv/tv-features/norm-macdonald-tribute-appreciation-1226839/.
- Itzkoff, David. "Sports Show Offers Comedian a Comeback," *New York Times*, April 5, 2011, https://www.nytimes.com/2011/04/06/arts/television/norm-macdonald-rises-again-on-comedy-central-sports-show.html.
- Kaplan, Michael. "My Lost Vegas Weekend With Norm Macdonald," *Esquire*, September 16, 2021, https://www.gq.com/story/norm-macdonald-gambling-vegas.
- Lakatos, Imre and Alan Musgrave (Eds.). *Criticism and the Growth of Knowledge. Proceedings of the International Colloquium in the Philosophy of Science, London, 1965*. Cambridge: Cambridge University Press, 1970.
- Loofbourow, Lili. "Norm Macdonald Never Stopped Bulls– tting," *Slate*, September 16, 2021, https://slate.com/culture/2021/09/norm-macdonald-death-anti-confessional-comic.html.
- Lucretius. *On the Nature of the Universe*. Latham translation, Penguin Classics, 1951.
- Macdonald, Neil. "Neil Macdonald on brother Norm's confessions of a cult leader," CBC, August 30, 2016, https://www.cbc.ca/news/entertainment/norm-macdonald-book-1.3740268.
- Macdonald, Norm. *Me Doing Standup*, Comedy Central Records, 2011,
- Macdonald, Norm. *Based on a True Story: Not a Memoir*, Random House, 2016.

- Macdonald, Norm. *Hitler's Dog, Gossip & Trickery*, Netflix, 2017.
- MacPherson, Guy. "What's So Funny?" with guest Norm Macdonald, July 2012, https://youtu.be/xxEwRaT9Xzw.
- Marchese, David. "Normcore: Norm Macdonald's Quest to Host 'The Late Late Show', *Rolling Stone*, June 2, 2014, https://www.rollingstone.com/culture/culture-news/normcore-norm-macdonalds-quest-to-host-the-late-late-show-68651/.
- Marchese, David. "Norm Macdonald Unloads on Modern Comedy, SNL, Fallon's Critics, Hillary, and Trump," *New York Magazine*, September 23, 2016, https://www.vulture.com/2016/09/norm-macdonald-book-snl.html.
- Marchese, David. "In Conversation: Norm Macdonald," *New York Magazine*, September 13, 2018, reprinted September 9, 2021, https://www.vulture.com/2021/09/norm-macdonald-in-conversation.html.
- Maron, Marc. "Episode 219 – Norm Macdonald". *WTF with Marc Maron* Podcast, October 17, 2011, http://www.wtfpod.com/podcast/repost-norm-macdonald-from-2011.
- Matthews, David. "Norm Macdonald Doesn't Like Where Stand-Up Comedy Is Headed," *Esquire*, September 26, 2016, https://www.esquire.com/entertainment/books/q-and-a/a48918/norm-macdonald-interview/.
- Mosbaugh, Erin. "Norm Macdonald Tweets The Story of When Bob Dylan Invited Him Over for Lunch," *First We Feast*, January 20, 2015, https://firstwefeast.com/eat/norm-macdonald-tweets-the-story-of-when-bob-dylan-invited-him-over-for-lunch/.
- Munroe, Grant. "Deadpan Walking," *The Walrus*, October 17, 2016, https://thewalrus.ca/deadpan-walking/.
- Nagel, Thomas. "What Is It Like to Be a Bat?", *Philosophical Review*, LXXXIII (4): 435–450, October 1974.
- New York Daily News, "Norm MacDonald remembers Steven Seagal as worst 'SNL' host ever," *New York Daily News*, September 23, 2016, https://www.nydailynews.com/entertainment/gossip/confidential/norm-macdonald-remembers-steven-seagal-worst-snl-host-article-1.2803798.

- O'Brien, Sherry. "The Norm Macdonald I remember…," *Chortle*, September 19, 2021, http://www.chortle.co.uk/correspondents/2021/09/19/49293/the_norm_macdonald_i_remember.
- Parker, Ian. "Norm Macdonald Talks Chekhov," *New Yorker*, October 10, 2016, https://www.newyorker.com/magazine/2016/10/17/norm-macdonald-talks-chekhov.
- Playboy. "20 Questions: Norm Macdonald," *Playboy*, August 1997, http://www.fakenews.net/archive/interviews/1997_08_playboy.html.
- Popper, Karl. *Conjectures and Refutations: The Growth of Scientific Knowledge*, 1963.
- Popper, Karl. "Natural Selection and the Emergence of Mind", *Dialectica*, vol. 32, no. 3-4, 1978, pp. 339-355.
- Power, Tom. "Interview with Norm Macdonald," *q with Tom Power*, CBC/Radio-Canada, October 27, 2016, https://www.cbc.ca/listen/live-radio/1-50-q/clip/10589127-norm-macdonald-sort-tells-truth-memoir.
- Rose, Nick. "'Death Doesn't Gnaw at Me': A Lost Interview With Norm Macdonald," *Rolling Stone*, September 17, 2021 [original interview in August 2018], https://www.rollingstone.com/tv/tv-features/norm-macdonald-lost-interview-1226722/.
- Ross, Jeff. "Jeff Ross Remembers Norm Macdonald," *Common Sense with Bari Weiss*, September 15, 2021, https://bariweiss.substack.com/p/jeff-ross-remembers-norm-macdonald.
- Roundtree, Cheyenne. "The Complicated Legacy of Norm Macdonald," *The Daily Beast*, September 25, 2021, https://www.thedailybeast.com/the-complicated-legacy-of-norm-macdonald.
- Rowan, Nic. "Norm Macdonald's Spiritual Journey," *First Things*, September 17, 2021, https://www.firstthings.com/web-exclusives/2021/09/norm-macdonalds-spiritual-journey.
- Ruby, Matt. "Norm Macdonald: The eyes of a child, the words of an adult," *Medium*, October 7, 2021, https://medium.com/vibe-

control/norm-macdonald-the-eyes-of-a-child-the-words-of-an-adult-f9f43f24b8c3.

- Russell, Lars. "Norm Macdonald and the Art of the Contradiction," *New York Magazine*, May 16, 2017, https://www.vulture.com/2017/05/norm-macdonald-and-the-art-of-the-contradiction.html.
- Rytlewski, Evan. "Norm MacDonald Talks Stand-Up, Teases FX "Reality" Show," *Shepard Express*, March 13, 2009, https://shepherdexpress.com/culture/ae-feature/norm-macdonald-talks-stand-up-teases-fx-reality-show/.
- Sauer, Abram. "Norm MacDonald Has No Problem Paying O.J. Simpson Under the Table," *Esquire*, April 12, 2011, https://www.esquire.com/entertainment/interviews/a9760/norm-macdonald-sports-show-5552106/.
- Schudel, Matt. "Norm Macdonald: Comedian whose dark jokes made him a TV favourite," *The Independent*, September 22, 2021. https://www.independent.co.uk/news/obituaries/norm-macdonald-comedian-obituary-death-b1923380.html.
- Shah, Beejoli. "Norm Macdonald Slams Bret Easton Ellis In Just 140 Characters," *Defamer*, October 15, 2013, https://defamer.gawker.com/norm-macdonald-slams-bret-easton-ellis-in-just-140-char-1445811019.
- Siegler, Mara. "Norm Macdonald isn't on his own dating app," *Page Six*, September 5, 2018, https://pagesix.com/2018/09/05/norm-macdonald-doesnt-know-how-to-use-his-own-dating-app/.
- Sims, David. "Norm Macdonald's Protective View of Comedy," *The Atlantic*, September 13, 2018, https://www.theatlantic.com/entertainment/archive/2018/09/norm-macdonalds-protective-view-of-comedy/570127/.
- Sims, David. "Norm Macdonald Wanted Laughter, Not Applause," *The Atlantic*, September 15, 2021, https://www.theatlantic.com/culture/archive/2021/09/remembering-norm-macdonald/620080/.
- Sorensen, Erick. "The Gospel According to Norm," *1517*, September 15, 2021, https://www.1517.org/articles/the-gospel-according-to-norm.
- Standard-Freeholder. "Comic legend Norm Macdonald had deep roots in North Stormont," *Standard-Freeholder*, September 20,

2021, https://www.standard-freeholder.com/news/local-news/comic-legend-norm-macdonald-had-deep-roots-in-north-stormont.

- Walther, Matthew. "Norm Macdonald's Comedy Was Quite Christian," *New York Times*, September 20, 2021, https://www.nytimes.com/2021/09/20/opinion/norm-macdonald-christian-comedy.html.
- Wild, David. "Norm Macdonald: Mr. Wrong," *Rolling Stone*, April 15, 1999, https://www.rollingstone.com/tv/tv-news/norm-macdonald-mr-wrong-180661/.

Printed in Great Britain
by Amazon

57213969R00059